Social Protection Floors

Social Protection Floors

Volume 3: Governance and Financing

Edited by Isabel Ortiz, Valérie Schmitt, Loveleen De

International Labour Organization

Cover photo:
© Portrait of young girls in the market of Puok, province of Siem Reap. Cambodia. ILO/N. Rain

Social Protection Floors. Volume 3: Governance and Financing
Isabel Ortiz, Valérie Schmitt, Loveleen De (Eds.)

© International Labour Organization 2016, Social Protection Department.
ISBN: 978-1-365-58589-0

We need to provide protection for people, all people, to allow them to leave a life without this never ending struggle.../... Support for this campaign is close to my heart. It promotes social justice through the development of national Social Protection Floors for all. It encourages the leaders of governments, trade unions, employers, non-governmental organizations in African countries and around the world, objectively, to engage in dialogue.

Desmond Tutu,
Archbishop Emeritus and Nobel Laureate

Social protection floors are an optimal public policy. They are an excellent social policy, much needed to reduce poverty and inequality. Social Protection floors are also a good economic policy, supporting household consumption, increasing human capital and thus productivity. All countries should be developing social protection floors; if adequately designed, they are affordable even in low income countries.

Jose Antonio Ocampo,
former United Nations Under-Secretary General,
former Minister of Finance of Colombia and
ILO Goodwill Ambassador

Acknowledgements

This book is the third volume of the series on "Social Protection Floors" published by the ILO. The editors would like to express their sincere thanks and gratitude to all the people who have contributed to this volume through their authorship, research and analysis. The different chapters of this volume are authored by and benefit from contributions by various people (in alphabetical order):

Aidi Hu, Senior Social Protection Specialist for East Asia, ILO; Alfredo Sarmiento; Anis Chowdhury, Consultant for the ILO; Bart Verstraeten, Political Secretary, Wereldsolidariteit-Solidarité Mondiale, Belgium; Carine Thibaut, Head of Campaigns Department, CNCD-11.11.11, Belgium; Clara van Panhuys, Social Protection Officer, ILO; Celine Peyron-Bista, Chief Technical Advisor, ILO; D Rajasekhar, Professor at the Institute for Social and Economic Change, India; Eduardo Méndez, Director of Centro de Estudios, Banco de Previsón Social, Uruguay; Frank Earl, former Executive Director, South African Social Security Agency; Geneviève Binette, Consultant for the ILO; Hans-Christoph Ammon, GIZ India; Joana Mostafa; Jurriaan Linsen, Consultant for the ILO; Lina Castaño, former Director of Productive Inclusion and Sustainability in the Department for Social Prosperity, Colombia; Lou Tessier, former Social Protection Officer, ILO Yangon; Lucia Mina Rosero; Malika Ok, Project Officer, ILO Phnom Penh; Maya Stern-Plaza, Legal Officer, ILO; Mies Cosemans, Responsible for Communication Campaigns, 11.11.11, Belgium; Namerta Sharma, GIZ India; Natália Sátyro; Netnapis Suchonwanich, former Deputy Secretary-General, National Health Security Office, Thailand; Pathamavathy Naicker, General Manager, South African Social Security Agency; Stefan Urban, Actuary, ILO; Thibault van Langenhove, Social Protection Policy Officer, ILO; Tomas Barbero, formerly of the ILO and Victoria Giroud-Castiella, Social Protection Officer, ILO.

The editors also value the support received from various people in reviewing the chapters (in alphabetical order):

Christina Behrendt, Senior Social Protection Specialist, ILO; Emmanuelle St-Pierre Guilbault, Senior Legal Specialist, ILO; Fabio Durán-Valverde, Senior Social Protection Specialist, ILO; Helmut Schwarzer, Senior Social Protection Specialist, ILO Mexico; Hiroshi Yamabana, Senior Actuary, ILO; Jeronim Capaldo, Senior Econometrics and Data Specialist, ILO; Kagisanyo Kelobang, Social Protection Specialist, ILO; Luis Frota, Senior Social Protection Specialist for Southern Africa, ILO; Markus Rück, Senior Social Protection Specialist for South Asia, ILO; Stefan Urban, Actuary, ILO; Thaworn Sakunphanit, Director of the Health Insurance System Research Office, Thailand; Victoria Giroud-Castiella, Social Protection Officer, ILO and Xenia Scheil-Adlung, Senior Health Protection Specialist, ILO.

Last but not the least, the editors express their gratitude to Jessica Vechbanyongratana, Assistant Professor at Chulalongkorn University, Thailand and Victoria Giroud-Castiella, Social Protection Officer, ILO for their support to the series on "Social Protection Floors".

The editors of this volume are Isabel Ortiz, Director of the Social Protection Department, ILO; Valérie Schmitt, Chief of Social Policy, Governance and Standards, ILO and Loveleen De, Social Protection Policy Officer, ILO.

Contents

x. Governance and Financing

List of figures

List of tables

Introduction

Social protection floors: A global consensus

Social protection allows for a life in dignity. However, it is still a privilege for far too few. Many older persons do not receive pensions and few children, mothers and persons with disabilities get the support that they need. Too many people are poor and without jobs, left behind by prosperous societies. This massive social protection gap is not acceptable from a human rights perspective. It is also a missed opportunity from a developmental point of view.

Access to social protection is not only a moral imperative, enshrined in the Universal Declaration of Human Rights and other international agreements, but also a critical ingredient for economic growth. Investing for an educated and healthy workforce can foster transitions from low productivity jobs to decent, high productivity jobs. Social protection serves as a stabilizer in times of crisis, providing much-needed income that can maintain or even boost demand and consumption during economic downturns. These positive impacts on workers and the resilience of national economies make social protection systems an attractive investment for many countries and one that will support them in their efforts towards sustainable economic growth.

In a time of rising inequalities, social protection is an indispensable tool for creating inclusive and equitable societies, in which redistribution and solidarity play important roles to build and maintain a lasting social peace.

It is for these reasons that social protection systems and floors are a key priority for the ILO and UN member States. In 2012, the Social Protection Floors Recommendation (No. 202) was adopted unanimously by ILO member States (see Annex 1). This Recommendation is the only internationally agreed treaty that reflects a global consensus on universal social protection. It defines social protection floors (SPFs) as a set of social security guarantees that ensure, at a minimum, that all people have access to social protection at adequate benefit levels – or income security. Social protection floors typically include, but are not limited to, cash transfers for children, maternity benefits, disability pensions, support for those without jobs, old-age pensions as well as access to essential health care.

The roll-out of social protection floors is one of the key priorities of the United Nations' 17 Sustainable Development Goals (SDGs), adopted by all countries across the world in 2015. The 2030 development agenda (see Annex 2) calls for efforts to eradicate poverty and equalize income distribution so that as countries continue to develop, the benefits of growth can be enjoyed by all. Specifically, SDG 1.3 commits States to implement nationally appropriate social protection systems and measures for all, including floors, by 2030.[1] By establishing universal social protection systems, including social protection floors, countries can ensure that no one is left behind and that prosperity is shared.

Since the end of the 19th century, significant progress has been made in building social security or social protection systems.[2] From early steps taken in a number of pioneering European countries, the scope of social security, measured by the number of areas covered by social protection systems,[3] was extended at

---

[1] Countries will track progress till 2030 on the proportion of population covered by social protection systems and floors, including coverage of women and men, children, unemployed persons, older persons, persons with disabilities, pregnant women, newborns, victims of work injuries, the poor and the vulnerable.

[2] In this series, social protection and social security are used interchangeably.

[3] Countries tend to build their national social security systems in sequential steps, depending on circumstances and priorities. In many cases, countries have first addressed the area of employment injury; followed by the introduction of old-age pensions, disability and

an impressive pace, including the creation of ministries of labour, ministries of social security and welfare and other relevant institutions. Today, the majority of countries have social protection schemes established by law as well as a myriad of cash transfers, albeit in many developing countries, the schemes benefit only a minority of the population.

Against this backdrop, countries across the world have prioritized the expansion of coverage. From a historical perspective, it is the right time. Today, India is richer than Germany was when it introduced social insurance for all workers in the 1880s and Indonesia is richer than the United States was when it enacted the Social Security Act in 1935. Many developing countries have successfully established universal social protection schemes, providing evidence to the rest of the world that expanding coverage to all is not only necessary but also feasible.

This is because social protection works. It is not a form of charity or a way of giving a few dole-outs to the most vulnerable. Social protection involves strategically designing and implementing comprehensive national systems. Such systems can raise productivity by investing in the workforce; ensure national consumption through higher incomes; and reduce poverty, inequality and political instability. In just a few years, China has put in place nearly universal pensions. Developing countries such as Argentina, Bolivia, Botswana, Brazil, Cabo Verde, Kazakhstan, Lesotho, Maldives, Mongolia, Namibia, Nepal, South Africa, Thailand, Timor Leste and Uruguay, among others, have established universal social protection schemes. Many governments are expanding the coverage of pensions for older

---

survivor benefits; and the later introduction of sickness, health-care and maternity coverage. Benefits for children and families and unemployment benefits are often implemented last (see the World Social Protection Report 2014-15. Geneva, ILO).

persons, disability and maternity benefits, support for people without jobs and cash transfers for children.

Most interestingly, developing countries are expanding coverage in very innovative ways. We try to reflect the richness of the new 21st century approaches in the volumes in this series.

About this volume: Governance and financing

This is the third volume of a series on successful experiences in building social protection floors. This volume showcases 20 experiences from 14 countries in the areas of participatory formulation of social protection strategies and design of schemes, transparent and efficient governance and innovative financing of social protection floors.

The development of SPFs is a multi-step process involving the formulation of a national social protection strategy, development of a strategy to finance social protection, design of institutional frameworks, development or reform of legal frameworks, and design and implementation of an efficient delivery mechanism and a monitoring and evaluation system.

According to Recommendation No. 202, this process should be based on national social dialogue involving governments, representative organizations of employers and workers as well as consultations with other relevant and representative organizations such as civil society and academia. Myanmar offers an interesting example of developing a social protection strategy based on an inclusive dialogue process. Tripartite partners and civil society organizations should be involved in the participatory design or reform of social protection schemes, including the exploring of possible financing options. Likewise, it is crucial to ensure that the delivery systems for SPFs are transparent and accountable and offer efficient and accessible complaint and appeal procedures. The development of a national culture of social protection can help to raise awareness among people and ensure that beneficiaries of SPFs become rights holders.

With regards to financing social protection systems, it is often argued that social protection is not affordable, or that government expenditure cuts are inevitable during adjustment periods. But there are alternatives, even in the poorest countries. There are eight options, supported by UN and IFIs policy statements: re-allocating public expenditures, increasing tax revenues, expanding social security coverage and contributory revenues, lobbying for aid and transfers, eliminating illicit financial flows, using fiscal and foreign exchange reserves, borrowing or restructuring existing debt, and adopting a more accommodative macroeconomic framework.[4] This volume presents examples on some of these innovative ways to finance social protection, such as through taxation of natural resources (Bolivia, Mongolia and Zambia), financial transaction taxes (Brazil), debt restructuring linked to social programmes (Ecuador), and the expansion of social contributions and removal of fuel subsidies (Indonesia). These are not minor sources of funding, on the contrary, these strategies can be used to finance large-scale social protection interventions; for example, Bolivia is financing a universal pension with a tax on hydrocarbons and Mongolia a universal child benefit with a tax on copper exports.

The volume also focuses on the legal and administrative aspects of governance. Brazil and South Africa have made the right to social protection legally enforceable and guaranteed social protection provisions for the long term. Many countries have implemented efficient and coordinated delivery mechanisms for their social protection floors. This includes shared registries and common identification systems to increase outreach and improve transparency, as seen in Brazil and Thailand. The Indian

---

[4] See Ortiz, I., Cummins, M. and K. Karunanethy. 2015. Fiscal Space for Social Protection: Options to Expand Social Investments in 187 Countries (Geneva, ILO).

RSBY smart card and database system could be used by other programmes in future. Colombia has a unified vulnerability assessment for social assistance while China, Mongolia, parts of India and South Africa have implemented stationary or mobile one-stop shops which provide information to people, register prospective beneficiaries, collect contributions and pay benefits. China improves compliance with social protection schemes through synergetic labour and social security inspections. Two countries namely Belgium and Uruguay have developed a national culture of social protection, which further strengthens the national consensus on social protection.

The achievements of different countries presented in this volume demonstrate that participatory design processes, rights-based legal frameworks, transparent and efficient delivery mechanisms, innovative and sustainable financing, as well as a national culture of social protection are important ingredients to successfully design and implement national SPFs. These experiences can serve as a source of inspiration to all countries that have prioritized the development of nationally appropriate social protection systems and measures for all, including floors, as part of their SDG implementation plans. The diversity of examples shows that there is no "one size fits all" approach to the development of universal social protection. Indeed, each country needs to find its own path in line with its vision of society. The number of country cases indicates that there is great scope for South-South exchange in the extension of social protection.

It is our hope that this volume will give readers concrete ideas on extending social protection to all and, in a few years, many more countries will be able to share their experiences with social protection policy makers from the Global South.

1

Belgium: Communication campaign[5]

In 2014, a coalition of Belgian civil society organizations launched the "Social Protection for All" national campaign to promote the human right to social protection. The aim of the Campaign is to raise awareness on the importance of social protection worldwide and convince Belgian and European policy-makers to take action to put the right to social protection for everyone across the world into practice.

Under the auspices of the two main umbrella organizations of the Belgian North-South movement, 11.11.11 (Dutch speaking Belgium) and CNCD-11.11.11 (French and German speaking Belgium), a group of trade unions, health mutual organizations and non-governmental organizations (NGOs) designed and implemented a campaign called "Social Protection for All". Both umbrella organizations have a longstanding tradition of developing awareness-raising campaigns and conducting joint advocacy work targeted towards Belgian decision-makers.

The starting point for the Campaign was the unacceptable fact that 73 per cent of the world's population does not enjoy access to comprehensive social protection.

---

[5] This chapter was authored by Mies Cosemans of 11.11.11, Carine Thibaut of CNCD-11.11.11 and Bart Verstraeten of Wereldsolidariteit-Solidarité Mondiale and reviewed by Isabel Ortiz, Victoria Giroud-Castiella and Valérie Schmitt of the ILO. It was first published in September 2016.

1. Main lessons learned

- The collaboration and coordinated action of a coalition of civil society organizations is a powerful tool to convince people and policy-makers of the importance of adequate social protection worldwide.
- The Campaign showed that communication and raising awareness on social protection are powerful tools to realize the right to social protection.
- While older generations are aware of the importance of social protection because they have enjoyed the continuous developments achieved over the last century, often newer generations take social protection for granted and are not aware of its importance. The Campaign was an opportunity to explain to the Belgian population that everyone should be concerned about social protection policies.
- The principle of the "right to social protection" received broad support. Many people understood that social protection is a basic prerequisite for a decent life.

2. Why is the "Social Protection for All" campaign needed?

The Campaign was developed and launched for two main reasons:

- Civil society organizations involved (trade unions, health mutual organizations and NGOs) found that there was very little knowledge amongst the Belgian population about the substantial lack of social protection in the world. A decision was therefore taken to conduct a large-scale awareness-raising campaign to highlight the challenges faced by people who do not enjoy adequate social protection around the world.
- In the past, Belgium has had a lead role in promoting the issue of social protection on the international agenda. Despite this track record, campaign partners are

convinced that the Belgian authorities could play an even greater and stronger role in the future. With the support of the wider public on this issue, the coalition seeks to ensure that social protection is firmly anchored in Belgian foreign policy.

Moreover, in Belgium, a high-income country, the issue of social protection remains a topical theme. Social protection guarantees, as in other European countries, are under increasing pressure. The Campaign is also an ideal opportunity to explain to the Belgian population that the struggle for comprehensive social protection policies is relevant in Belgium and in many other countries, as highlighted by the 2030 Agenda for Sustainable Development.

3. How does the Campaign work?

The design of the Campaign started in 2014 with a seminar to develop the key strategic lines. Key UN experts, including from ILO and the then UN Special Rapporteur on the Right to Food participated in the seminar. Soon after, campaign partners agreed on one vision and a joint working definition of social protection as a sound basis for the two-year Campaign, which is largely inspired by ILO standards in the field of social protection, particularly the Social Security (Minimum Standards) Convention, 1952 (No. 102), and the Social Protection Floors Recommendation, 2012 (No. 202).

The Campaign aims to:
- raise awareness amongst the general public about the importance of social protection and make them aware of the fact that billions of people in the world lack access to social protection; and
- put pressure on Belgian and European policy-makers to give social protection a central role in foreign policy.

The target groups are:
- the general public;
- Belgian and European policy-makers;

- the members and supporters of the different campaign partners; and
- children and adolescents attending primary and secondary education.

To develop the advocacy agenda and the awareness-raising materials, the partners' coalition established two different working groups. An advocacy working group wrote a powerful dossier on social protection worldwide, calling for "solidarity-based social protection, by all, for all". It also developed a manifesto to gather the institutional support of other Belgian civil society organizations for the Campaign. By the end of 2015, a total of 56 Belgian civil society organizations signed up to the campaign manifesto.

A campaign working group developed the materials and communication tools to make the general public aware of the importance of social protection worldwide:

- a common website containing information on the Campaign and all the materials developed;
- a documentary about social protection in Bolivia, Senegal and Belgium as well as an interactive game on developing a social protection system. They were awarded three prizes.
- photos and film documenting the contrast between those who enjoy social protection and those that are excluded in Mali;
- a video collecting testimonies from persons deprived of social protection in the Global South and experiences to facilitate and promote access to social protection;
- educational materials for primary and secondary schools: (i) campaign partners developed an education toolkit, including a board game, about social protection and lesson tips for teachers; (ii) 11.11.11 commissioned a theatre company to produce a musical on the topic of social protection, thereby bringing the subject to the children's level; (iv) CNCD-11.11.11 made an exhibition with cartoons which travelled the country. On their

request, a theatre company produced a play about social protection in Belgium and internationally. It played extensively in schools, training centres and cultural centres. (v) an action day was organized in schools. The coalition called on many schools to host awareness-raising actions, thereby putting the Campaign in the spotlight. Hundreds of actions brought thousands of pupils into contact with the Campaign;

- a video clip that was broadcast on national television reaching hundreds of thousands of people; and
- a compelling movie that, through creative word play, highlighted social protection. The message was: "Solidarity and caring for one another. In society we leave no one behind, we turn our back on no one."

In the first year of the Campaign, the coalition of partners tried as much as possible to get people to express their support for social protection for all. To that end, a specific plaster was developed with the slogan "Social Protection for All", which people were invited to stick somewhere on their body before taking a selfie and uploading it on the Campaign's website.

Initially, the communication materials were used by all Campaign partners to convey the same message. In the second year, each partner had the freedom to focus on a specific topic relating to social protection. 11.11.11 has chosen to highlight health care in the South. CNCD-11.11.11 has worked on the link between free trade negotiations and social protection. The common advocacy working group remains deeply committed to embedding the principle of social protection in Belgian foreign policy.

With the support of partners in the South, the coalition launched a global call to action on social protection. To that end, they developed a visual "world map of actions" undertaken by civil society organizations around the world to promote solidarity-based social protection. It is a strong signal for politicians that people and civil society worldwide want solidarity-based social protection for all. Every added action increases the power of the Campaign. These actions are gathered on a separate website. With operations in Belgium and throughout the world, the Campaign can convince politicians of the need for adequate social protection worldwide.

4. **What are some of the impacts of the Campaign?**

- In May 2016, the Belgian Federal Parliament adopted a resolution that requests the Belgian Government to give a clear and central place to social protection in Belgian international policy. As a result, the Federal Public Service on Social Security has concluded a cooperation agreement with the Belgian Development Agency to put their expertise at the disposal of third countries seeking support.
- More than 40,000 people posted self-clicked photographs to express their support for social protection for all.
- Guy Ryder, ILO Director General, expressed his support for the Campaign at the Belgian Federal Parliament in December 2015 and called upon the Belgian Government to support social protection worldwide.
- A total of 56 Belgian civil society organizations expressed their support for the Campaign by signing the manifesto.

The principle of the right to social protection received broad support. Many people understood that social protection is a basic need for a decent life.

5. **What are the challenges?**

The Campaign will officially finalize its activities in December 2016. Its legacy is a full package of tools and communication materials. The major challenge is the appropriation of these materials and the Campaign's message by civil society in Belgium in order to continue raising awareness and advocating for the extension of social protection.

6. References

A collection of testimonies from the South about the consequences of not having access to social protection. Available at: http://socialebescherming.be/campagne/zuidverhalen.aspx (in Dutch) and www.protectionsociale.be/-du-nord-au-sud-et-vice-versa- (in French).

Education toolkit including a board game about social protection, lesson tips for teachers. Available at: http://www.11.be/kom-in-actie/op-school/secundair/item/eerste-hulp-bij-Onderwijs-koffer (in Dutch) and www.cncd.be/mallette-pedagogique-protection-sociale-pour-tous

Multimedia project concerning social protection in the world including a film and an interactive game for the general public. Available at: www.bienvenueaprovidence.com/

Film footage about the contrast between enjoying social protection and having none at all in Mali. Available at: www.youtube.com/watch?v=M2IFU2QsC7s.

Exhibition of cartoons about social protection. Available at: www.cncd.be/Expo-de-caricatures-Kroll

Global action for social protection. Website. Available at: http://socialprotection.world/.

Social Protection for All. Website of the Campaign. Available at: www.protectionsociale.be/ (in French) and www.socialebescherming.be (in Dutch).

Solidarity and caring for one another. In society we leave no one behind, we turn our back on no one. Video (in Dutch). Available at: www.youtube.com/watch?v=1mlMcM_-pH4.

Solidarity-based social protection, by all, for all: Manifesto. (English version, Spanish version, French version). Available at: http://socialprotection.world/manifesto.aspx.

Television clip that was broadcast on national television reaching hundreds of thousands of people (in Dutch). Available at: www.youtube.com/watch?v=u0FozcoMlo4.

2

Bolivia: Financing social protection through taxation of natural resources[6]

Bolivia is a an example of how countries with natural resources can create fiscal space to expand social protection and generate government revenues to support social and socio-economic development and to help mitigate inequality and reduce poverty.

Bolivia's annual economic growth averaged 4.9 per cent between 2004 and 2014, with poverty rates falling from 59 per cent in 2005 to 39 per cent in 2014. The Gini index fell from 0.6 to 0.47 in the same period, while social spending increased significantly, as indicated in Figure 1. Bolivia's development over the last decade is closely linked to policy changes regarding its natural resource extractive industries.

---

[6] This chapter was authored by Stefan Urban of the ILO and reviewed by Isabel Ortiz and Hiroshi Yamabana of the ILO. It was first published in August 2016.

Figure 1: Bolivia's public investment spending (in US$ millions, nominal) and annual GDP growth (in %)

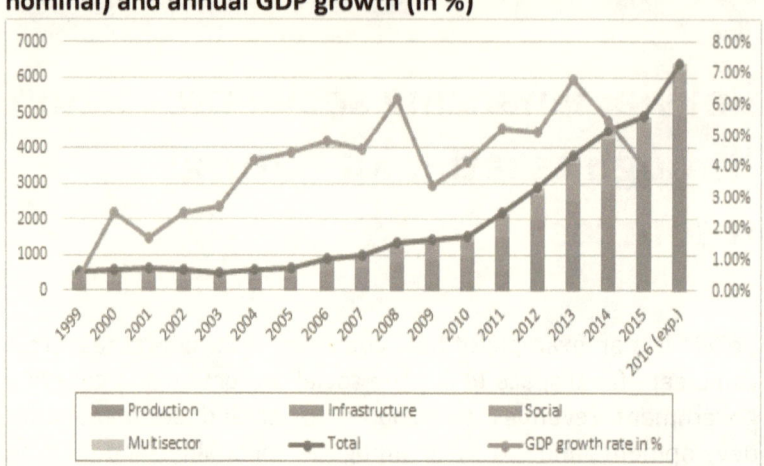

1. Main lessons learned

- Natural resource rich countries can boost their social protection system through the taxation of natural resources, increasing government revenues and supporting the expansion of social protection expenditures.
- Earmarking government income generated from natural resources can directly link the allocation of funds to social protection programmes.
- The process of increasing social expenditures was accompanied by a transparency initiative that requires local and national governments to disclose their revenues and transfers. Civil society organizations in parallel carry out monitoring of company payments to the State and the management of related revenue at the national and subnational levels.
- Through the taxation of natural resources and the expansion of social protection spending, the Government managed to reduce poverty rates and inequality, while also supporting economic growth.

2. Natural resource extraction tax and global trends

Adjusting the taxation of extractive industries is a strategy many countries have used to increase fiscal space. Due to the rise of commodity prices during the past decade and a sharp increase in profits among the world's largest mining companies, a number of governments around the world have reviewed their shares in the distribution of the rents. The United Kingdom increased the supplementary tax on oil production in 2011, and the Government of Australia, against heavy opposition from the booming mining sector, introduced a mineral resource rent tax of 22.5 per cent in 2012.

Countries around the world are revising the regulatory environment for extractive industries. In recent years, discussions among different stakeholders on reforming tax and ownership regimes took place in Brazil, the Democratic Republic of the Congo, India, Mali, Mozambique, the Philippines, South Africa and the United States. In South Africa, for instance, there have been extensive debates on the nationalization of the mining sector, with the conclusion that a fairer redistribution of mining profits can be achieved through the introduction of a resource rent tax of 50 per cent and the creation of a state mineral company to develop strategic minerals.

While developed economies have a broad base to collect taxes and social security contributions to finance social protection, developing countries often struggle to generate government revenues through taxation and contribution collection. Tax authorities tend to be weak and taxation systems often lack transparency, while a relatively large share of the population is employed in the informal sector, making it difficult and costly to collect social security contributions and income taxes. This also limits the means for redistributive policy to reduce inequality and poverty.

In many developing countries, collecting higher public revenues through rents from natural resources and extractive industries is of particular importance for the financing of development. Developing countries can raise revenues either by directly extracting the natural resources through a state-owned enterprise, joint-ventures or other forms of co-extraction, or by selling the exploitation rights and taxing the profits of a single industry. Both avenues can provide revenues for social and socio-economic development.

3. Taxing hydrocarbons in Bolivia

Bolivia is the second largest supplier and largest exporter of natural gas in South America. Over the past 10 years, natural gas production in Bolivia increased from 2.8 billion cubic metres in 1998 to 13.9 billion cubic metres in 2008. Hydrocarbon revenues contributed to 35 per cent of the country's GDP and 55 per cent of total exports in 2013.

Orthodox neoliberal policies in the 1980s resulted in the majority of the extractive industries being privatized and in the hands of foreign companies. Producers earned high profits, but paid little in royalty payments, leading to widespread dissatisfaction among the Bolivian population. The widespread dissatisfaction initiated an activist movement and the so-called "Gas Wars" that led to the resignation of President Sánchez de Lozada and a national referendum on the regulation of the distribution of hydrocarbon wealth. The previous share of 82 per cent of oil revenues for the producers and 18 per cent for the State was equalized at a 50-50 split. Bolivia introduced stronger state control starting in 2003 with the introduction of a direct tax on hydrocarbons (IDH) and with the renegotiation of contracts. Revenues from IDH and royalties increased from US$338 million in 2004 to over $726 million in 2005. In 2006, the newly elected president, Evo Morales, "nationalized" Bolivia's oil and gas sectors and changed state royalties to 80 per cent, thus greatly increasing government revenues from the sector. Government revenues rose from $1.55 billion in 2006 to $2.7 billion in 2008 and to $6 billion in 2014. Taxing hydrocarbons became a key to Bolivia's national and, in particular, social development

As of 2006, Yacimientos Petroliferos Fiscales Bolivianos (YPFB), the country's national oil company, was the only entity authorized to undertake activities in the exploration and sale of hydrocarbons. YPFB, consisting of mostly state-owned subsidiary companies, administers service contracts with international companies, including British Gas, Canadian Energy Enterprise, Pluspetrol, Bolivia Corporation S.A., Petrobras, Repsol YPF, Total and Vintage Petroleum. Investors initially threatened to take legal measures against the Bolivian State and to freeze their investments, but as the Government still offered attractive returns even after the new measures, most of them eventually signed the new agreements without legal actions.

Another measure that contributed to Bolivia's success in creating fiscal space for social and socio-economic development is the revenue transparency initiative that requires local and national governments to disclose their revenues and transfers. Civil society organizations carry out monitoring of company payments to the State and the management of related revenue at the national and subnational levels, thus supporting the oversight of government finances and the efficiency of social spending. All the rules regulating resource revenue sharing with subnational authorities, including earmarking provisions and transfers to subnational authorities, are available online and for public consultation.

4. Hydrocarbon taxation and social protection

A portion of revenue from hydrocarbon taxation is earmarked for a universal old-age pension scheme, Renta Dignidad, and additional portions are directed to other cash transfer programmes, such as the Bono Juancito Pinto, for schoolchildren. Public spending increased in all areas, with a particularly high increase in social spending.

The Bono Juancito Pinto is a cash transfer in Bolivia whose beneficiaries are children going to public schools. It was established in 2006 with the aim of reducing dropout rates among students enrolled in government schools. They were provided with an annual grant of 200 Bolivia Bolivianos (BOB) ($25) conditional on their attendance at school. Financing came entirely from the additional 32 per cent share that YPFB had in total revenues from the hydrocarbon sector. In 2007 and 2008, YPFB and the state mining consortium (COMIBOL) financed 47 per cent of the programme and the treasury provided the remaining funds. In 2010, 1.6 million children received the Bono Juancito Pinto at a cost of $54 million, about 0.24 per cent of Bolivia's GDP.

From 1997 to 2007, Bolivia had non-contributory benefits provided through Bolivida and Bonosol for people over 65 years of age. In 2007, a new programme called Renta Dignidad was created, replacing Bonosol, providing universal social income for people over 60 years of age. The programme started in 2008 and pays an annual benefit of $340 for people without a pension income, and 75 per cent of that amount to people with another existing pension. The programme is funded using up to 30 per cent of all IDH revenues, as well as from dividends from renationalized companies.

5. Conclusion

The increase in taxation on the oil and gas industry enabled the Government of Bolivia to generate sizeable rents that are transferred to sectors and regions with developmental needs and supports the extension of social protection measures. Universal social pensions and other cash transfer schemes, such as the Renta Dignidad and the Bono Juancito Pinto programme, are financed through earmarked hydrocarbon tax revenues. Bolivia, thanks to its extractive industries, has managed to significantly reduce poverty and inequality, while also guiding its economy towards a positive development path, with annual growth rates averaging around 4.9 per cent since 2004.

Taxing natural resource extraction is one of the many alternatives that countries have to expand fiscal space for social protection. Governments normally use a mix of taxes and social security contributions to fund social protection, combined with other options explained in the paper, "Fiscal Space for Social Protection: Options to Expand Social Investments in 187 Countries".

6. References

Aresti, M. L. 2016. Oil and gas revenue sharing in Bolivia, Revenue sharing case study, (Natural Resource Governance Institute).

Boadway, R; Flatters F. 1993. The taxation of natural resources – Principles and policy issues, Policy Research working papers No. WPS 1210 (Washington, DC, World Bank).

Center for Economic and Policy Research (CEPR). "Bolivia`s economy under Evo in 10 graphs", in The Americas Blog. Available at: http://cepr.net/blogs/the-americas-blog/bolivias-economy-under-evo-in-10-graphs [31 Aug. 2016].

Ernst, C. Forthcoming. Revenues from extractive industries: An opportunity to finance sustainable social spending (Geneva, International Labour Organization).

Ministry of Planning and Development. 2016. Inversión Sectorial (La Paz). Available at: www.vipfe.gob.bo/index.php?opcion=com_contenido&ver=cont enido&id=2189& id_item=704 [31 Aug. 2016].

Ortiz, I.; Cummins M.; Karunanethy K. 2015. Fiscal space for social protection: Options to expand social investments in 187 countries, ESS Working Paper No. 48 (Geneva, International Labour Office).

Stratfor. 2015. Bolivia`s natural gas sector is under threat. Available at: https://www.stratfor.com/analysis/bolivias-natural-gas-sector-under-threat [31 Aug. 2016].

United National Conference on Trade and Development (UNCTAD). 2014. Trade and Development Report, 2014 (New York and Geneva, United Nations).

3

Brazil: Cadastro Único[7]

Operating a registry through a national public bank: The Cadastro Único database covers one third of Brazil's population. Cadastro Único could progressively be used as the reference registry for the whole social protection system (including contributory schemes).

Officially created in 2001, Cadastro Único is a shared registry for Brazil's vulnerable population, defined as households earning half of the minimum wage per capita (about US$170 per month).

Operated by a public bank, Caixa Econômica Federal, Cadastro Único is consistent with Brazil's decentralization efforts. The registry provides municipalities with clear roles and responsibilities, minimizes data collection efforts, and ensures consistency and efficiency of the social protection system.

The single registry's main client is the Family Grant (Bolsa Família) programme. Bolsa Família disbursed more than 13 million payments per month in 2013.

1. Main lessons learned

- The collection and compilation of data on Brazil's poor and vulnerable population has enabled local governments and policy-makers to develop a better

---

[7] This chapter was authored by Thibault van Langenhove of the ILO, and Joana Mostafa and Natália Sátyro of Cadastro Único and reviewed by Isabel Ortiz, Valerie Schmitt, Helmut Schwarzer and Fabio Durán of the ILO. It was first published in October 2014.

understanding of this population and develop appropriate and coordinated programmes.

- The installation of a single registry for the poor population operated by a federal bank has increased social assistance programme outreach and mitigated the risks of data manipulation, fraud, and clientelism. This arrangement provides service providers with consistent targeting and automatic payments to beneficiaries without intermediaries. It has also enabled beneficiaries to clearly understand their eligibility for various programmes and to easily claim benefits (98 per cent of the delivered benefits are withdrawn within one month).
- Progressive adjustments and improvements to the single registry have allowed for better transparency and traceability of the social protection system, notably through online access and automatic controls with other existing administrative databases.

2. The need for a unique and shared database on the poor population

Social assistance programmes targeting the poor and vulnerable have a long history in Brazil. Previously, each programme had its own tools and processes for collecting data and identifying beneficiaries. Registries were kept separate even within the same ministry or agency. As a result, the social protection landscape was scattered and inconsistent, which resulted in limited outreach and numerous inclusion/exclusion errors (partly as a result of fraud). The abundance of small databases and the absence of a consolidated database also led to a lack of information on poor populations and, consequently, to their invisibility to policy-makers.

Taking stock of the situation in 2001, the Government decided to consolidate four different cash transfer programmes targeting poor and vulnerable families and create a unique national registry. The consolidation was executed in 2003. The goals of

Cadastro Único are to identify poor families, develop an understanding about their characteristics, and geo-reference poor households.

Since the outset, Cadastro Único has been part of the Government's national social protection strategy focused on poverty eradication (Plano Brasil Sem Miséria) to identify poor populations and their needs and centralize all this information in a single registry.

3. **A single registry covering about 78 million people and operated by a federal bank**

Cadastro Único targets Brazil's vulnerable population, which is defined as families who earn at or below half of the minimum wage per capita (US$6 per day or US$170 per month). The 2010 census led to the identification of 20 million low-income families in Brazil (67 million people or 35 per cent of the total Brazilian population). The registry contains data for over 23 million families.

The federal bank, Caixa, has been in charge of operating the single registry since the outset. The bank was selected mainly because of its large network of agencies (including national lottery shops), its experience with managing large databases, and its ability to handle the 13.8 million monthly payments targeted by Cadastro Único with no delays.

Data collection and data entry is done by the 5,570 local governments (municipalities) in Brazil. The software for data entry was developed on demand by Caixa. The latest version, launched in 2010, includes online access, which has helped to solve consistency and synchronization issues between the local governments' systems and the central Government database.

Data validation and cross-checking is the responsibility of the federal Government which guarantees harmonization and coherence across municipalities.

Figure 2: Registration process for Brazil's Cadastro Único

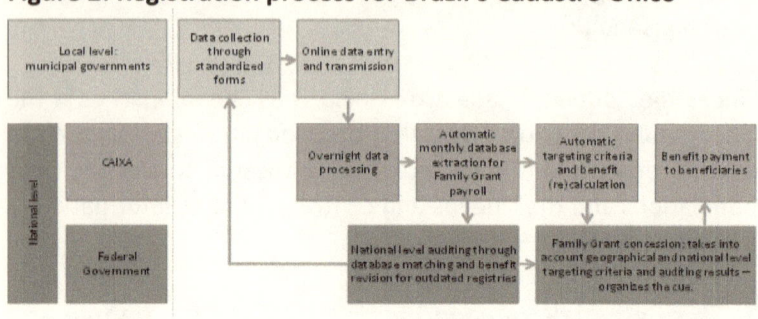

The process to register in Brazil's Cadastro Único and receive the Family Grant, one of the main benefits delivered using the single registry, is explained in Figure 2. Coverage increased from 6 million families in 2003 to 11 million families in 2006 and 13.9 million in 2013. The bold expansion of the Family Grant brought the single registry's flaws and inconsistencies into the spotlight. Most of the issues were the result of two pitfalls:

- the technical fragility of the data collection form, which had been developed without seeking expertise on social programmes or questionnaire and survey techniques;
- the low quality of data inherited from previous existing databases.

To overcome these challenges, the Ministry of Social Development, in association with the Brazilian Institute of Geography and Statistics and the Applied Economics Research Institute, organized a debate on the data collection form from 2005 to 2007. These discussions have resulted in an improved and more consistent form (similar to the national census and the household survey forms), as well as better capacity building initiatives (manual and training) at the local level.

To reduce inclusion errors, a data verification process has been installed, which systematically matches entries with other administrative records.

4. **The single registry is part of Brazil's decentralization process and has resulted in more consistent pro-poor policies**

Cadastro Único has facilitated the development of in-depth knowledge about the poor population, greatly improving the ability of local and central governments to formulate and implement appropriate policies for the poor.

From an operational aspect, Cadastro Único has considerably improved the consistency of social welfare policies: all programmes now use common targeting criteria and tools to select their beneficiaries and a common delivery mechanism for cash benefits.

The use of the single registry has also contributed to the improvement of the transparency and traceability of information: all data are available online and, in the first quarter of 2013, 98 per cent of benefit payments were performed automatically through the payroll system.

Benefit cancellation is also automatic and is regulated and controlled by the central Government.

Finally, the implementation of Cadastro Único has empowered subnational authorities in the management and delivery of social protection programmes through providing them with concrete roles and responsibilities. In order to ensure the quality of the database, the programme includes incentives for municipalities to keep data updated.

5. **What's next?**

The main challenge facing Cadastro Único remains the maintenance of such a large database on vulnerable populations. It is particularly complex since the single national Management Information System does not yet cover local-level registration and analysis needs. Hence, local-level managers often duplicate data, resulting in synchronization issues and data security problems, or deviate from the original purpose of the centrally defined processes to match their local needs.

Connectivity and system availability are remaining challenges for the Cadastro Único. Even though an online solution is ideal, the stages of local government institutional and economic development are not homogeneous, making it complex to implement an online system and utilize the system on a daily basis.

From a development perspective, the registry could be used as the reference registry for the whole social protection system (including contributory schemes). Maintaining a larger database will be even more challenging, but should result in savings for the social protection system as a whole through resource pooling, increase the efficiency of identifying beneficiaries, and facilitate the implementation of social protection floors covering the whole population.

6. References

Assis, S.A.G.; Ferreira, J. 2010. "Usos, potencialidades e limitações do Cadastro Único no subsídio às políticas sociais para a população de baixa renda", in J. Abrahão de Castro and L. Modesto (eds.): Bolsa família 2003-2010: Avanços e desafios/organizadores (Brasília, IPEA).

Barros, R.P.; Carvalho, M.; Mendonça, R.S.P. 2010. "Sobre as utilidades do Cadastro Único", in J. Abrahão de Castro and L. Modesto (eds.): Bolsa família 2003-2010: Avanços e desafios/organizadores (Brasília, IPEA).

Barros, R.P. et al. 2008. A importância das cotas para a focalização do Programa Bolsa Família, Niterói: Faculdade de Economia, Universidade Federal Fluminense Texto para Discussão, No. 238.

Ministério do Desenvolvimento Social e Combate à Fome do Brésil. 2005. Sistema Único de Assistência Social – SUAS. and Norma Operacional Básica NOB/SUAS. Available at: www.mds.gov.br/bolsafamilia/cadastrounico.

Cunha, R. 2009. "Transferência de renda com condicionalidade: A experiência do Programa Bolsa Família", in Concepção e gestão da proteção social não contributiva no Brasil (Brasília, Ministério do Desenvolvimento Social e Combate à Fome and UNESCO).

Sátyro, N.; SOARES, S. 2009. "Diagnóstico e desempenho recente do Programa Bolsa Família", in Brasil em desenvolvimento: Estado, planejamento e políticas públicas (Brasília, IPEA).

Soares, F.; Ribas, R.; Osório, R. 2007. Evaluating the Impact of Brazil's Bolsa Família: Cash Transfer Programmes in Comparative Perspective, IPC Evaluation Note, No. 1.

Soares, S. 2012. Bolsa Família, Its Design, Its Impacts and Possibilities for the Future. IPC Working Paper, No. 89.

Vieira, A. 2009. "Sistemas de informação e gestão do Programa Bolsa Família e do Cadastro Único de Programas Sociais do Governo Federal", in Concepção e gestão da proteção social não contributiva no Brasil. (Brasília, Ministério do Desenvolvimento Social e Combate à Fome and UNESCO).

4

Brazil: Financing social protection through Financial Transaction Taxes[8]

Brazil offers an excellent example of how financial transactions taxes (FTTs) can be used to generate revenues for public provisioning of social services while concurrently mitigate financial instability arising from short-term capital flows.

A financial transaction tax is a small tax levied on various types of financial instruments, such as shares, bonds, foreign currency transactions, derivatives and bank debits and credits. The FTTs are implemented in at least 40 developed and developing countries. Ten European Union countries are expected to adopt FTTs in January 2017. The existing rates vary from a maximum of 2 per cent to as low as 0.00001 per cent.

FTTs have a dual goal of raising revenues while discouraging the type of short-term financial speculation that has little social value and poses high risks to the economy. One estimate shows that FTTs can generate US$2.9 to $14.5 billion in all developing countries combined depending on their design (coverage or base and rate) and the size of their financial sectors.

FTTs are easy to administer by existing authorities with no new institutions required. It also can be highly progressive as it allows resources to be channelled directly from the formal economy to those who need social protection.

---

[8] This chapter was authored by Anis Chowdhury and reviewed by Isabel Ortiz, Jeronim Capaldo, Hiroshi Yamabana and Stefan Urban of the ILO. It was first published in August 2016.

1. Main lessons learned

- FTTs in Brazil contributed to the collection of nearly $20 billion in additional government revenues per year.
- The Government earmarked income generated through FTTs directly to funding for social protection programmes (health care (42 per cent), social insurance (21 per cent), Bolsa Família cash transfers (21 per cent) and other social services (16 per cent)).
- FTTs assisted Brazil in consolidating the health system. The largest proportion of FTT revenue is earmarked for health care.
- The FTTs helped Brazil to expand its social protection services and contributed to the reduction in inequality. The Gini coefficient fell by 5.2 points and the percentage of households living below the poverty line halved between the early 1990s and 2008.
- FTTs serve a dual purpose both to encourage certain types of market behaviour (such as longer term investments) and as a revenue raising mechanism.
- Contrary to what is often communicated, there is no evidence of adverse impacts of FTTs on the financial markets.

2. FTTs in Brazil

Brazil first introduced a bank debit tax in 1993, but it was short-lived. The longest lasting bank debit tax – Contribuicao Provisoria sobre Movimentacao ou Transmissao de Valores e de Creditos e Direitos de Natureza Financiera (CPMF) – was put in place in 1997 at an initial rate of 0.20 per cent. The rate increased gradually starting in 1999 (0.22 per cent) to 0.38 per cent in 2002. Revenues raised from the CPMF were originally earmarked to finance health-care programmes (0.2 per cent), to combat poverty (0.1 per cent) and for social assistance (0.08 per cent). The CPMF collected nearly $20 billion per year.

The CPMF was discontinued by the Senate in 2008 after the Supreme Court ruled that earmarking revenue from such taxes was unconstitutional. The CPMF was replaced by a higher tax rate for financial firms (Social Contribution on New Corporate Profits) of 15 per cent, but the tax was repealed in 2013.

According to an International Monetary Fund (IMF) report, the CPMF raised about three times the amount raised by the corporate income tax (CIT) on financial companies. As can be seen from Table 1, the bank debit tax, or CPMF, was a significant source of tax revenue accounting for 7.4 per cent of total taxes collected in 2001.

Table 1: Gross revenues from bank debit tax in Brazil

		Gross revenue	
Year	Tax rate	% of GDP	% of tax revenue
1994	0.25	1.06	3.6
1997	0.20	0.80	2.8
1998	0.20	0.90	3.0
1999	0.22	0.83	2.9
2000	0.34	1.33	4.8
2001	0.36	1.45	7.4
2002	0.38	NA	6.1
2003	0.38	1.48	NA

The financial operations tax (IOF), a second component of FTTs introduced in 1999, subjected capital inflows for portfolio investments and investments in local assets to a 2 per cent tax to be paid at the point of the settlement date in Brazilian reals. That is, the tax is paid when foreign currency is converted into Brazilian reals.

According to the Government, the IOF tax is designed to offset the impact of short-term capital inflows on the Brazilian real. Thus, the rate was raised subsequently to slow the appreciation of the Brazilian currency and to prevent speculation in the

Brazilian stock and capital markets when the United States pursued expansionary monetary policy in response to the 2008-09 global financial crisis.

The Government increased the IOF rate to 0.38 per cent in 2008 on several financial transactions involving foreign exchange, loans and insurance. Since 2009, the IOF has been levied at the rate of 5.38 per cent on foreign loans, where the average payment term of the loan is lower than 90 days. For loans with an average payment term higher than 90 days, the IOF rate is now 0.38 per cent. Increases in the IOF rate compensated for the loss of tax revenue caused by the abolition of the CPMF in 2008.

In June 2015, Brazil slashed the IOF from 6 per cent to zero to prevent sharp depreciation of the Brazilian real against the US dollar with the normalization of the market and the upward adjustment of the US interest rate. However, this adjustment will have a significant impact on government tax revenues, especially when the economy slows down.

Therefore, in December 2015, Brazil's Congress approved the 2016 Budget which calls for the creation of a tax over financial transactions (CPMF tax). According to the Finance Minister of Brazil, Joaquim Levy, if the CPMF was not approved, certain important programmes, such as unemployment benefits and workers' protection, would be at risk.

3. FTTs and social protection

As the CPMF was designed mainly to finance social protection expenditures, the mechanism was classified as a "social contribution". During the period in which the CPMF was in place, 42 per cent of the revenue collected was used for the public unified health system, 21 per cent for social insurance, 21 per cent for Bolsa Família (conditional cash transfers) and 16 per cent for other social purposes. By 2007, total revenue from the CPMF amounted to 1.4 per cent of GDP, enough to cover the total cost of Bolsa Família and other non-contributory social protection programmes. This represents how other developing countries can raise their own revenues to help finance public services. The Gini coefficient fell by 5.2 points and the percentage of households living below the poverty line halved between the early 1990s and 2008 when notable legislative and programmatic changes were made in the economic and social policy sphere, including increasing the minimum wage and public expenditures on health, education and social services.

4. Assessment

One estimate shows that Brazil could potentially raise $227 million per year from FTTs. Brazil also successfully earmarked revenues for use by local governments to fund health programmes. CPMF revenues rose from approximately 0.8 per cent to 1.3 per cent of GDP in 1997-99 and 2000, respectively. In terms of total tax revenues, the CPMF increased from 2.8 per cent in 1997 to 7.4 per cent in 2001 (Table 1). Thus, there seems to be very little leakage or avoidance. From the experiences of other countries, it seems that Brazil's success is likely due to three factors. First, the latest CPMF rate was not excessively high. Second, the Brazilian banking system is relatively sophisticated and widely used for payments. Third, the CPMF was levied on bank debits only, rather than on both debits and credits. This highlights how the implementation details affect success and the importance of setting appropriate rates.

There is no evidence of adverse impacts of the CPMF on the financial market. However, there is consistent evidence that the CPMF altered financial and investment behaviour, especially in the wake of its introduction at the end of January 1997. Between January and February 1997, demand deposits increased by almost 40 per cent as the introduction of the CPMF reduced the opportunity cost of holding funds in non-interest-bearing demand deposits.

Evidence on incidence is mixed. The bank debit tax was progressive in that it affected those with bank accounts, which is a minority in the wealthiest group of the population. One study found that the incidence of the tax was approximately proportional over the entire income distribution, making the tax neither progressive nor regressive. Another study, using household consumption data and the incidence of the FTT through the price system, found that it fell proportionately more on lower income families.

5. Conclusion

Brazil is an important example of an FTT regime in a developing country with a relatively large financial sector. Between 2000 and 2005, the CPMF accounted for more than 8 per cent of total expenditures on social protection, which shows just how important it was in financing social protection. In particular, revenue raised through CPMF assisted Brazil to consolidate the health system as the largest proportion of FTT revenues was earmarked for health-care programmes. During the early 2000s, Brazil collected about 37 per cent of GDP in taxes and spent 8.4 per cent of that on health. Thus, government expenditures on health care represented 3.4 per cent of GDP.

FTTs serve a dual purpose both to encourage certain types of market behaviour (such as longer term investments) and to raise revenue. However, Brazil's on and off episodes with FTTs display the resistance that such taxes can face from vested interests, especially in the powerful financial sector.

There are some concerns that FTTs may harm the poor, especially those dependent on remittance income from abroad. A group of international finance experts hold the view that it is highly unlikely that the cost of a small tax of say 0.005 per cent on such transactions, which would amount to a tax of just 5 cents on a $1,000 transfer, would be passed on to the retail customer. Furthermore, the poor are highly unlikely to be engaging in the high-speed speculative trading activities that are the target of these taxes. Moreover, remittances can be exempt from FFTs if required.

FTTs are becoming easier to administer as technological advancements facilitate this type of tax collection. A number of developing countries have already implemented some form of tax on financial transactions and the IMF believes that such taxes can generate substantial revenues.

Taxing financial transactions is one of the many alternatives that countries have to expand fiscal space for social protection. Governments normally use a mix of taxes and social security contributions to fund social protection, with other options (Ortiz et al, 2015).

6. References

Coelho, I. 2009. Taxing bank transactions: The experience in Latin America and elsewhere, presented at III ITD Conference Beijing (Washington, DC, Inter-American Development Bank).

Coelho, I.; Ebrill, L.; Summers, V. 2001. Bank debit taxes in Latin America: An analysis of recent trends, IMF Working Paper Fiscal Affairs Department (Washington, DC, IMF).

Grabel, I. 2005. "Taxation of international private capital flows and securities transactions in developing countries: Do public finance considerations augment the macroeconomic dividends?" in International Review of Applied Economics, Vol. 19, No. 4, pp. 477-497.

Lavinas, L. 2014. A long way from tax justice: The Brazilian case, Global Labour University Working Paper No. 22 (Geneva, ILO and Berlin, Global Labour University).

Ortiz, I.; Cummins, M.; Karunanethy, K. 2015. Fiscal Space for social protection: Options to expand social investments in 187 countries, ESS Working Paper No. 48 (Geneva, International Labour Office).

Holmes, R.; Hagen-Zanker, J.; Vandemoortele, M. 2011. Social protection in Brazil: Impacts on poverty, inequality and growth (London, Overseas Development Institute).

Paes, N.L.; Bugarin, M.N.S. 2006. "Reforma tributária: Impactos distributivos, sobre bem-estar e a progressividade", in Revista Brasileira de Economia, Vol. 60, No. 1, pp. 33–56.

Suescun, R. 2004. Raising revenue with transaction taxes in Latin America: Or is it better to tax with the devil you know? World Bank Policy Research Working Paper 3279 (Washington, DC, World Bank).

Stijn, C.; Keen, M.; Pazarbasioglu, C. (eds). 2010. Financial sector taxation: The IMF's report to the G-20 and background material (Washington, DC, IMF).

World Health Organization (WHO). 2004. Tax-based financing for health systems: Options and experiences, Discussion Paper No. 4 (Geneva).

Zockun, Maria H. 2007. A regressividade da CPMF in Informações FIPE, December.

5

Brazil: Anchoring rights in law[9]

The adoption of the 1988 constitution marked a landmark in the history of the Brazilian social security system by introducing a universal social security model grounded in citizenship rights. The Constitution sets out the State's responsibility in organizing and legislating social security. This should be done according to principles of universality of protection, adequacy of benefits and with the objective of ensuring the uniformity and equivalence of benefits and services for urban and rural populations. In the last few decades, Brazil has taken bold steps to build and maintain a comprehensive social protection system that reinforces basic social rights.   Of notable example is the legislation of programmes to assist families in overcoming hunger and poverty.

1. Main lessons learned

- Brazil's experience shows that the constitution can play a pivotal role in establishing comprehensive social protection when it sets out the right to social security, the architecture of the social security system and a benchmark for the level of contributory benefits.
- Law is an essential tool for securing social protection entitlements and extending social protection coverage.
- By establishing legal entitlements and making rights enforceable, the law can shape the human right to social security.

---

[9] This chapter was authored by Maya Stern Plaza and Geneviève Binette of the ILO and reviewed by Isabel Ortiz, Valérie Schmitt, Helmut Schwarzer and Emmanuelle St-Pierre Guilbault of the ILO. It was first published in September 2016.

- Social security systems grounded in law contribute to sustainable development and poverty reduction beyond the initiative of a single government.

2. The right to social protection in the Brazilian constitution

Brazil's social protection system finds its legal foundation in the 1988 constitution, which is recognized for its extensive inclusion of social rights, including the right to social security. "Education, health, nutrition, labour, housing, leisure, security, social security, protection of motherhood and childhood" are guaranteed as social constitutional rights (article 6). In addition, the constitution paves the way for the development of a comprehensive social protection system by setting out the elements that make up the architecture of the system and by laying down guiding principles. It is the Government's constitutional obligation to establish the social security system by law along three pillars: health, social insurance, and social assistance (article 194). These pillars should be developed according to the objectives of universality, equivalence of benefits between urban and rural population, irreducibility of benefit amounts and diversity of methods and approaches, including of financing mechanisms (article 194). The constitution calls for the coverage of the population against the risks faced throughout the life cycle for both contributory and non-contributory schemes (articles 201, 203).

3. Legal architecture of the Brazilian social protection system

A. Access to health care

Built upon Articles 196-200 of its federal constitution, Brazil introduced the National Health System (Sistema Único de Saúde (SUS)) 25 years ago by adopting the Organic Health Law in 1990

(No. 8.080) with a view to reach universal health coverage and therefore give effect to the constitutional right to health.

The system is tax financed and provides medical services directly to patients in rural and urban areas including: general, specialist, maternity and dental care; hospitalization; medicine; and necessary transportation. It is accompanied by the Farmácia Popular programme established by Law 10.858 in 2004, which provides 112 medicines for common illnesses for free (e.g. diabetes and hypertension, among others) and another 11 with some cost sharing. The Ministry of Health ensures overall supervision of the SUS. The implementation of the health system has led to a significant drop in child mortality (according to the World Bank, 57.6 per cent from 1990 to 2008), leading the Ministry of Health to say that they had achieved the Millennium Development Goals for infant and child mortality before the 2015 target. However, despite the existence of a national tax-financed health system, a large part of health expenditures is still out-of-pocket (according to WHO, nearly 31 per cent in 2011).

B. Social protection for children and families

As part of the social assistance pillar set out in the constitution and the Organic Social Assistance Law 8742 of 1993, the Bolsa Família programme is the most significant income transfer programme in Brazil. It is aimed at reducing inequalities and breaking the inter-generational transmission of poverty, in particular among poor and extremely poor families, by promoting access to health, education and other welfare public services. Launched in 2003 by means of Provisional Measure 132, it was institutionalized when converted into Law 10.836 in 2004 at the same time as the establishment of the Ministry of Social Development and Hunger Eradication (MDS). This was the first of many legal instruments that were adopted in support of the formal organization of Bolsa Família, including Decree No. 5.209 that regulates Law 10.836. As part of its parameters, Law 10.836 establishes eligibility criteria, the benefit value, payment procedures and qualifying conditions. In addition, it sets outs the delivery mechanism as well as enforcement provisions, including sanctions in case of fraud. Details regarding the targeting process and the level and payment of benefits are provided by Decree No. 5.209. While the Bolsa Família covered approximately 3.6 million families at its creation in 2003, in 2015 it reached nearly 14 million households in all municipalities (48 million persons), representing about one quarter of Brazil's population (MDS). Its cost is estimated at only 0.5 per cent of GDP (MDS).

In 2011, the Brasil sem Miséria (Brazil without Extreme Poverty) was launched following the adoption of Decree No. 7.492. It widens and deepens the focus of Bolsa Família by providing a cash transfer to large families and to pregnant women, as well as introducing an additional income guarantee known as the poverty Superation Benefit. In addition, the programme promotes improved coordination with other non-contributory programs. The Brazil sem Miséria has a multilayer approach that also includes employment support benefits.

In line with Brazil's constitution, the scheme for private sector employees also provides family benefits to low-income employees with one or more children younger than 14 years of age according to Law 8.213 of 1991 regarding the General scheme. Since 2015, benefits were also extended to domestic workers and the self-employed. Benefits are provided to one or both parents so long as they are in insured employment or receiving a sickness benefit. Benefits are conditional on vaccination certificates and school attendance. The allowances are paid directly by the employers and reimbursed by the National Social Security Institute. Benefits are adjusted annually according to changes in the consumer price index.

C.   Social protection for women and men of working age

Although Bolsa Família primarily targets families with children, it should be noted that families in extreme poverty may qualify even if they do not have children. Alongside enhancing access to public services, such as health, social assistance, food security, education and housing, the Brazil sem Miséria also promotes social inclusion through facilitating labour market integration, providing training and fostering smallholder agriculture, among other initiatives. By 2014, this programme met its goal of lifting 16 million people out of extreme poverty and is currently in its second phase.

Brazil's contributory scheme provides sickness and maternity benefits, work injury benefits as well as disability and survivors' benefits to private sector employees and civil servants, including rural workers, domestic workers, some categories of casual workers and self-employed persons. The federal constitution established the contributory benefit programmes, in particular article 40 (public servant schemes) and article 201 (General Regime for the private sector). The particular details of the benefits are provided through Law 8.212 and Law 8.213 on social security. In addition, Law No. 7.998 of 1990 regulates unemployment insurance for persons employed in the formal private sector, but also other categories of workers, such as household workers and fishermen. Self-employed persons, however, are not covered. Law 9.717 sets out the entitlements and parameters concerning public servants.

An interesting feature of Brazil's social insurance system is its rural social insurance model given the extent of the country's agricultural sector (employing 18 million people, according to the FAO). This hybrid scheme, contributory in nature but significantly subsidized by the Government since its inception in the early 1970s, aims at addressing the unique needs of the rural sector. In line with the principle of equivalence set out in the constitution, the rural social insurance scheme, established by Laws Nos. 8.212 and 8.213 following the amendments introduced by Law 11.718 in 2008, provides disability and survivors' pensions, as well as maternity, work injury and sickness benefits.

The scheme covers three situations:
1. wage earners of large rural farms;
2. self-employed farmers that meet the criteria for small peasants; and
3. small peasants who work with family members on a plot of land smaller than four fiscal modules.

Where necessary, contributions are based on the percentage of sold production.

A. Social protection for older women and men

In accordance with article 203 of the federal constitution, the Continued Social Assistance Benefit (Benefício de Prestação Continuada or BPC) is a non-contributory scheme that provides a cash amount equivalent to the minimum wage for the elderly living in extreme poverty. The BPC therefore benefits from a constitutional legal status. The BPC is further legislated by Law No. 8742.

In line with the constitution (articles 201 and 202), the old-age contributory pension system is composed of three pillars: the General Social Security pay-as-you-go mandatory scheme for private sector employees legislated by Laws No. 8212 and 8213; a Pension Regime for Government Workers set out in Law 9.717; and a supplementary private pension system. As part of the first two pillars, salaried workers in industry, commerce and agriculture, as well as rural, domestic and casual workers, elected civil servants and self-employed persons are covered in case of survival beyond the age of 65 (men), 60 (women, male rural workers and civil servants) or 55 (female rural workers and civil servants).

The constitution details certain parameters in article 202 that govern the private pension supplementary system, including its voluntary nature, right to information and the need to be regulated by law. Complementary Laws No. 108 and 109 regulate the general rules and those regarding the state-run pension funds, respectively.

Following a reform in 2013, persons with disabilities are now covered through a new legal retirement scheme that responds to their special needs in line with the constitution and the UN Convention on the Rights of Persons with Disabilities.

4. Towards a comprehensive social protection legal framework based on international social security standards

Brazil is moving towards developing a comprehensive legally entrenched system providing protection throughout the life cycle. This is done by providing four basic social security guarantees that form the social protection floor set out in Recommendation No. 202, as well as higher levels protection set out in other ILO social security instruments.

Figure 3: Brazil's social protection legal framework

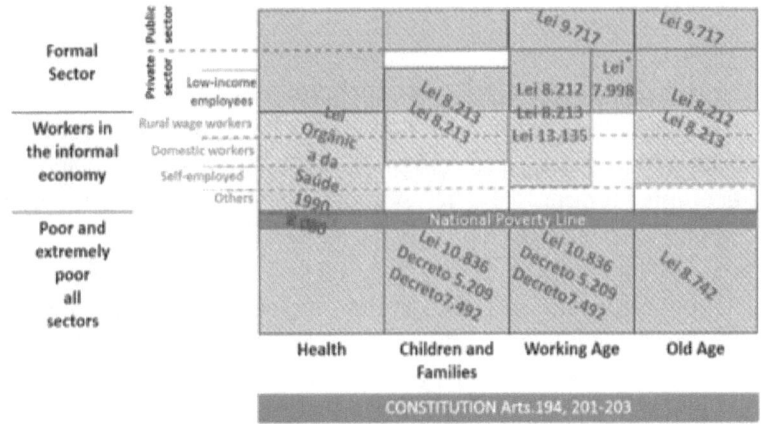

Access to health services are granted through a universal health-care scheme. Income security for families with children is ensured through contributory family benefits, the non-contributory Bolsa Família cash transfers and the Brasil sem Miséria programme. Income security for persons of working age is also guaranteed through contributory unemployment, maternity, sickness, employment injury, invalidity and survivors' benefits along with measures aimed at facilitating labour market integration, including through non-contributory schemes. Families in extreme poverty also qualify for Bolsa Família even if they do not have children. Finally, both contributory and non-contributory schemes provide older persons with income security.

Among the 96 ILO Conventions ratified as of 2015, Brazil is one of seven countries to have accepted all nine branches of the Social Security (Minimum Standards) Convention, 1952 (No. 102), in June 2009. It is also one of eight countries to have ratified the Employment Promotion and Protection against Unemployment Convention, 1988 (No. 168), in 1993, and is a State party to the Maternity Protection Convention, 1952 (No. 103), since 1965, and the Equality of treatment (Social Security) Convention, 1962 (No. 118), since 1969. The ratification of these Conventions is known to promote, solidify and sustain social protection rights.

The comprehensive and legally anchored Brazilian social security architecture has been commended for its efforts in extending social protection according to ILO standards, including Recommendation No. 202, notably by the supervisory body charged with monitoring ILO social security instruments.

The development and successful implementation of Brazil's comprehensive legal framework is furthered by the distinct prominence and culture of social dialogue around social protection. For example, a quadripartite (government, workers, employers and pensioners) National Social Protection Council was established by Law 8.213 and meets monthly to discuss, deliberate on and publish about relevant issues. Coupled with the extensiveness of detailed social protection provisions in the constitution, Brazil has paved the way for ensuring the extension of social protection through a comprehensive legal and institutional framework in line with the principles of universality of protection and coherence with social and employment policies as established by ILO instruments and other UN Conventions.

5. References

Gragnolati, M.; Lindelow, M.; Couttolenc, B. 2013. "Twenty years of health system reform in Brazil: An assessment of the Sistema Unico de Saude", in Directions in development: Human development (Washington, DC, World Bank).

ILO. 2011. General survey concerning social security instruments in light of the 2008 Declaration on Social Justice for a Fair Globalization, Report III (Part 1B), Social Security and the Rule of Law.

—. 2012. Social Security and Food Security: Successful Policy Experiences in Brazil, ESS Paper No. 30, http://www.ilo.org/wcmsp5/groups/public/---ed_protect/---soc_sec/documents/publication/wcms_207666.pdf.

—. 2014. World Social Protection Report 2014/2015 (Geneva). Available at: http://www.ilo.org/global/research/global-reports/world-social-security-report/2014/lang--en/index.htm.

—; WHO. 2010. Social Protection Floor Initiative: Brazil in search of universal protection. Available at: http://www.ilo.org/wcmsp5/groups/public/---ed_protect/---soc_sec/documents/publication/wcms_secsoc_17509.pdf.

ILO (FORLAC). 2014. Policies for the formalization of micro and small enterprises in Brazil. Available at: http://www.ilo.org/wcmsp5/groups/public/---americas/---ro-lima/documents/publication/wcms_318209.pdf.

ILO News. 2014. Formalizing employment in Brazil: A "simple" path to formal employment. Available at:

www.ilo.org/global/about-the-ilo/newsroom/features/WCMS_312067/lang--en/index.htm.

SSPTW. 2013. Brazil.

UNDP. "Brazil: Broadening social protection and integrating social policies", in Volume 18: Successful Social Protection Floor Experiences. Available at: http://tcdc2.undp.org/GSSDAcademy/SIE/Docs/Vol18/SIE_v18_ch3.pdf.

—. "Brazil: The Rural Social Insurance Programme", in Volume 18: Successful Social Protection Floor Experiences. Available at: http://tcdc2.undp.org/GSSDAcademy/SIE/Docs/Vol18/SIE_v18_ch4.pdf.

UNDP (International Policy Centre for Inclusive Growth). 2015. Social protection systems in Latin America and the Caribbean: Brazil, One pager No. 273. Available at: www.ipc-undp.org/pub/eng/OP273_Social_Protection_Systems_in_Latin_America_and_the_Caribbean_Brazil.pdf.

United Nations Economic Commission for Latin America and the Caribbean (ECLAC). 2013. Social protection systems in Latin America and the Caribbean: Brazil. Available at: http://repositorio.cepal.org/bitstream/handle/11362/4062/S2013126_en.pdf?sequence=1.

6

China: Community services[10]

In recent decades, China has rapidly extended social protection to a large number of people through various mechanisms, including social protection community services (SPCS).

SPCS include two types of services:
- **Access to social protection and active labour market policies (ALMPs), including scheme registration and benefit payments:** Services are made available within residential communities, thereby simplifying and expediting access to social protection.
- **Social and home-based services, such as health care and domestic assistance:** Services help older persons, people with disabilities and children to live independently, in safety and in dignity.

A growing number of residential communities provide SPCS as an essential component of their community services (CS). In 2014, a total of 311,000 community organizations provided a wide range of services, including SPCS, to residents in 45 per cent of urban communities (MOCA, 2014, 2015). In addition, some rural villages also provide these services.

1. Main lessons learned

- Making social protection administrative services accessible within communities can improve coverage, especially for people who are self-employed,

---

[10] This chapter was authored by Aidi Hu of the ILO and reviewed by Isabel Ortiz, Valérie Schmitt and Loveleen De of the ILO. It was first published in May 2016.

unemployed, outside the workforce or have no formal work contract.

- In China where the services sector is not fully developed and many households cannot afford expensive private services, social protection provides not just income security, but also services like medical care and domestic assistance to older persons, people with disabilities and vulnerable groups.
- SPCS facilitate employment generation by providing training and generating public and private services in the care economy.
- SPCS are public services, serving the lowest administrative units i.e. communities. They are supervised by the government and enforced through partnerships between the public and private sectors and civil society, with non-governmental organizations (NGOs) playing an ever increasing role.
- The expansion of SPCS is facilitated by China's Five-Year Plan 2016-20, which emphasizes increasing household income and consumption, universal social protection and development of the services sector.

2. What do SPCS consist of?

SPCS were initially introduced in a few Chinese regions in the late 1980s. Given their effectiveness and efficiency in responding to the emerging needs of residents, SPCS became a national policy supervised by the Ministry of Civil Affairs (MOCA) in close cooperation with others. However, no standard package of SPCS is imposed, allowing each community to decide on which services to provide, in line with its own needs and supply capacities. However, two types of services are generally included, as shown in Figure 4.

Figure 4: Services provided by SPCS in China

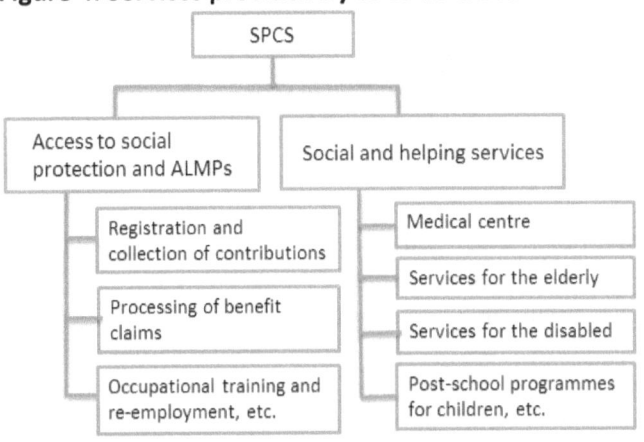

Access to social protection and ALMPs can be illustrated by the experience of people in Xiangtan district in Hunan Province. Residents no longer have to visit various district administrative offices, which are often located in areas far from their homes, to register for schemes, make inquiries and claim benefits. These functions can now be done within the community, irrespective of the type of benefit sought and the responsible agency (SIA Bureau of Xiangtan, 2015).

Examples of SPCS-provided social services include:
- general medical services provided twice a week by a doctor in the Puhui community;
- shopping and other necessary assistance for older residents and those with disabilities by a team of 128 volunteers in Mingchunyuan community;
- regular social activities for persons with disabilities in Shuangliu and Jichang communities; and
- an after-school programme for children, developed jointly by the Lead Social Workers' Group and Yayuncun community.

SPCS are also found in some rural villages. For instance, Xiazhai village with its 1,058 residents runs a home-based care programme for all of its 228 people above 60 years of age. The programme consists of free meals twice a day, live-in rooms at a very low price and regular medical attention. Similar programmes can be found in most of the 300 other villages in Jindong District of Jinhua City (CCTV-4, 2015).

3. **What are the major features of SPCS?**

- **Leadership and guidance:** The development of CS, including SPCS, is guided and supervised by the Government in support of several official documents, such as the Five-Year Plan 2011-15 (State Council, 2011) and the Guidance on Improving Community Services for Disabled Persons prepared jointly by 14 ministries in 2000.

- **Autonomy and responsiveness:** To a large extent, each community decides the content, scope, delivery, and financing of benefits provided. Given the autonomy and flexibility, as well as the knowledge that communities have about their own needs and financing capacities, communities can respond promptly to emerging requirements with a set of targeted SPCS.

- **Convenience:** Through SPCS, social protection administrative services are grouped together and made accessible within residential communities even when they belong to different ministries. This facilitates participation in and effective coverage of social protection. It is particularly important for the coverage of children, older persons and working-age people with no job, no stable job or no employer. It is estimated that about half of 731 million urban residents fell into these categories in 2013 (NBS, 2015).

- **Multiple resources:** SPCS are supported by multiple financial and human resources from the government, autonomous neighbourhood committees, volunteers, NGOs, charities and the private sector.[11] Of these,

---

[11] Each residential community consists of autonomous neighbourhood committees whose residents perform administrative functions.

volunteers have become a growing and indispensable force. According to the Civil Affairs Bureau of Beijing, there were 1.35 million and 1.5 million registered volunteers in Beijing in 2013 and 2014, respectively.

- **Coordination:** Close cooperation and partnership among public, private and civil society organizations at the community level contribute to the success of SPCS. Within a decentralized office, a shared database makes it possible to provide all the relevant benefits and services to beneficiaries, thereby allowing local administrators to improve coordination and the quality of public services for the people.

- **Employment generation:** Due to the development of SPCS and other types of community services, over 1 million jobs were created in residential communities in 2011 (MOCA, 2011).

Figure 5: Coverage of CS and SPCS in China, 2010-14[12]

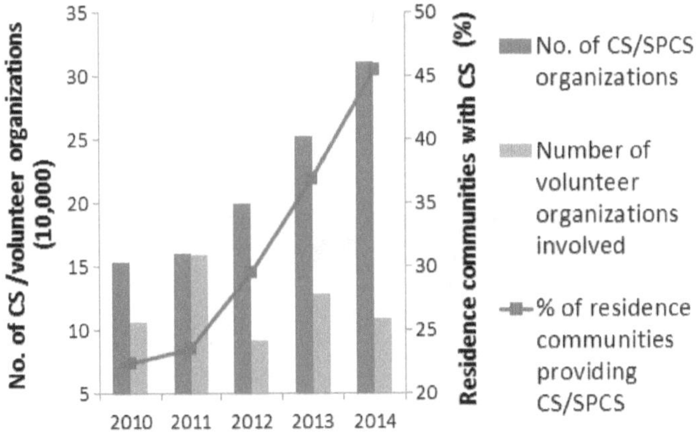

Source: MOCA, 2010-14.

The popularity of CS and SPCS has stimulated further development of community organizations as important service providers (see Figure 5).

---

[12] Volunteer organizations are civil society organizations or NGOs whose members usually belong to the residential communities.

4. Why are SPCS needed?

The main reasons why SPCS are needed include:

- The impacts of the one child policy combined with the ageing population and growing urbanization (see Figure 6) have reduced the capacities of families to provide regular care to older family members or those with disabilities, as was the traditional practice. The situation is more acute for rural families as working-age members often migrate to cities for work, leaving elderly parents and young children behind in remote villages.

- The reform of State Owned Enterprises (SOEs) released them from the responsibility of taking direct care of their employees, former employees and their families in all aspects of family life, such as education, health care and housing. These responsibilities had to be reassigned.

Figure 6: Ageing and urbanization in China, 1982-2013

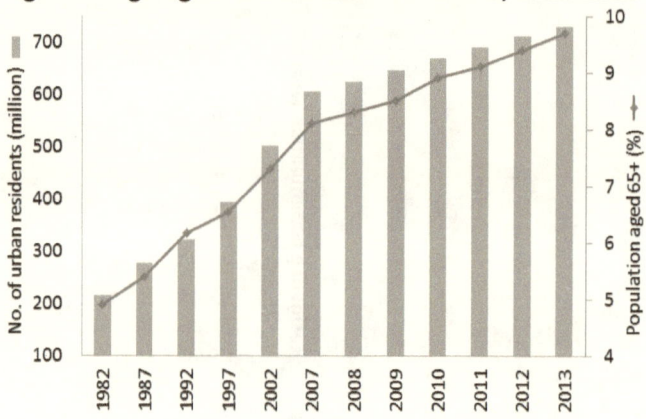

Source: National Bureau of Statistics of China (NBS), 2015.

- The services market in China is underdeveloped. To cite an example from Guangdong, the supply of institutional beds for older persons as a share of total elderly people was only 1 per cent, while 17.5 per cent of older people wanted to live in institutions (WCFA of Guangdong, 2010).

- To realize the goal of making basic universal social protection a reality, decentralized and convenient social protection services became necessary.

5. What's next?

China's experience demonstrates the crucial role of SPCS in the large-scale and quality extension of social protection. SPCS are expected to grow further in the future as the number of people above 60 years of age increases from 200 million currently to 300 million by 2025 and 400 million by 2033 (NWCFA, 2012 & 2015).

The expansion of SPCS is further facilitated by China's Five-Year Plan 2016-20, which places an emphasis on increasing household income and consumption, universal social protection and development of the service sector.

6. References

Central Committee of Communist Party of China. 2015. 中共中央关于制定国民经济和社会发展第十三个五年规划的建议 [Opinions on fomulating the 13th Five-Year Plan for National Economic and Social Development] (Beijing).

CCTV-4 (Chinese International Official Channel 4). 2015. 远方的家（273）[Our homes in distance, No. 273] (Jinhua). Available at: https://www.youtube.com/watch?v=NEWE0RCnO-o.

China Disabled Persons' Federation. 2015. 2014年中国残疾人事业发展统计公报 [Statistical bulletin on the development of the undertakings for disabled people in 2014] (Beijing).

Liu, Chuanyan & Xu, Genshen. 2012. 人口老龄化背景下社区老人服务需求现状调查研究 [Survey report on the needs of old people for community services] (Beijing).

MOCA. 2011-2015. 2010至2014年社会服务发展统计公报 [Statistical Bulletins on the development of social services, 2010–2014] (Beijing).

—; et al. 2000. 关于加强社区残疾人工作的意见 [Guidance on the Improvement of Community Services for Disabled Persons] (Beijing).

NBS. 2015. 中国统计年鉴 2014 [China Statistical Yearbook 2014] (Beijing).

NHFPC (National Health and Family Planning Commission). 2015. 中国家庭发展报告2015 [National report on the family development for 2015] (Beijing).

NWCFA (National Working Committee for Aging Issues). 2012. 2013年底中国老年人口总数将超过2亿[The number of old people will exceed 200 million by the end of 2013] (Beijing).

SIA (Social Insurance Administration) Bureau of Xiangtan. 2015. 个人参保缴费查询、养老金发放情况查询等业务下沉到街道(乡镇)人力资源和社会保障经办窗口办理 [Administrative services like checking contribution payment and claiming for pensions are now accessible from all urban and rural communities of Xiangtan] (Hunan).

State Council. 2011.中国老龄事业发展"十二五"规划 [The 12th Five Year Plan for the Development of the Old-Age Related Undertakings] (Beijing).

—. 2011. 社区服务体系建设规划（2011-2015年）[Development plan for the development of community services over 2011-2015] (Beijing).

WCFA (Working Committee for Aging Issues) of Guangdong. 2010. 广东老年人数过一千万，**养老床位占老年人**1% [The number of old people exceeds 10 million in Guangdong, but the number of institutional beds for the elderly is only about 1 per cent] (Guangzhou).

Yang, Zhijin [杨志锦]. 2015.**十三五重点**产业清单：服务业未来 占比有望达55% [List of the most important industries for 13th Five-Year Plan: the service sector is likely to amount to 55 per cent of GDP by the end of 2020] (Beijing).

7

China: Labour and Social Security Inspection[13]

Due to the Labour and Social Security Inspection (LSSI) mechanism in Qingdao city, 43,000 additional workers have been covered by social insurance over 2012-14.

Qingdao in Shandong Province is an east coast city, home to 9 million residents, including 2.87 million urban workers (QBS, 2015). Like other cities in China, extending basic social protection coverage to all workers and residents is among the development goals of Qingdao.

1. Main lessons learned

- Qingdao's experience demonstrates that an effective LSSI mechanism can help to extend social protection coverage, particularly to self-employed workers, migrant workers and those working in small or rural enterprises.
- Limited human resources is a long-standing challenge faced by the Inspectorate of Qingdao. One of the ways that the Inspectorate addresses this issue is by using innovative technology-based LSSI tools.

---

[13] This chapter was authored by Aidi Hu of the ILO and reviewed by Isabel Ortiz, Valérie Schmitt and Loveleen De of the ILO. It was first published in September 2016.

- Innovative tools do not only increase the capacity of the inspectorates, but also make it more pro-active in preventing and addressing compliance issues. In this way, the social security rights of workers are better protected and fulfilled.
- The experience of Qingdao shows the importance of a unified information system for the LSSI, such as the Integrated Database on Human Resources and Social Security (IDHRSS) of Qingdao. The database, which links LSSI tools and facilitates the collection of pertinent data, plays a fundamental role in ensuring the rights of workers.

Figure 7: Violations defined in Qingdao city's LSSI Regulation

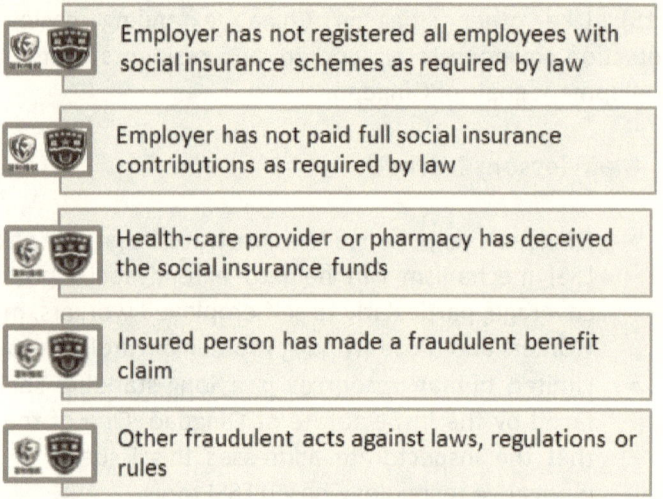

Employer has not registered all employees with social insurance schemes as required by law

Employer has not paid full social insurance contributions as required by law

Health-care provider or pharmacy has deceived the social insurance funds

Insured person has made a fraudulent benefit claim

Other fraudulent acts against laws, regulations or rules

2. Mandate for social security inspection

The Inspectorate of Qingdao was set up in 1994 and is responsible for all inspections related to employment and social security, as well as enforcement of compliance within its jurisdiction. With regards to social security inspection, five types of violations are defined in the city's LSSI Regulation.

3. A shortage of manpower

Despite a clearly defined mandate, the Inspectorate does not have sufficient manpower for executing the mandate. For instance, in 2015 it had around 150 full-time inspectors (Meng, 2015) while there were 161,000 working units and 2.87 million workers (QBS, 2015).

Figure 8: Lack of inspectors in Qingdao city

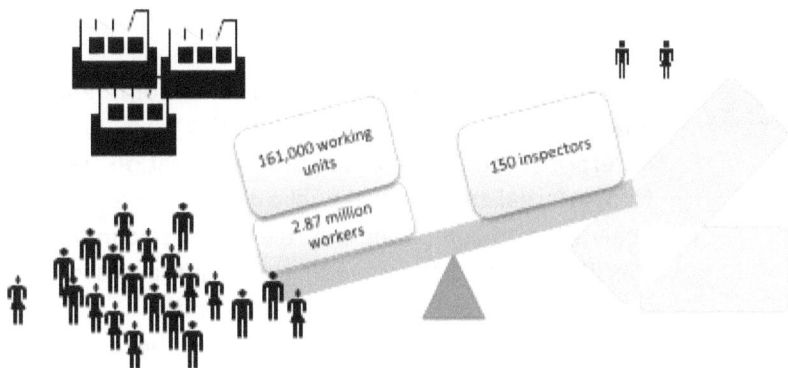

4. Technology-based LSSI tools

Given the limited number of inspectors and the large and ever-increasing number of businesses, the Inspectorate decided to resort to a series of technology-based innovations. Of them, three are briefly described below.

A. Twin Networks Management (TNM)

TNM is based of grid-based management (GBM) and network-based management (NBM).

The GBM is a human resource management tool that helps to allocate inspectors to enterprises. First, the GBM divides

Qingdao enterprises and workers into a grid of 396 groups and assigns an inspection team to each group (Meng, 2015). The responsibilities of these teams are to collect data from enterprises, provide legal and other information to employers and workers, inspect enterprises and enforce compliance.

Thanks to this decentralized approach, the Inspectorate has obtained support from local communities. In 2015, 300 part-time inspectors were provided by the local communities and 650 inspection assistants were recruited through government procurement services (Meng, 2015).

The NBM is a data management with three functions:
- collecting data for the IDHRSS, a comprehensive information system which includes all types of enterprise- and worker-related information received from internal and external public databases;
- analysing and comparing the relevant data contained in the IDHRSS to identify existing violation cases and the potential risks for further inspection; and
- based on the data analysis, classifying the enterprises into different compliance categories so that the inspection process can be prioritized.

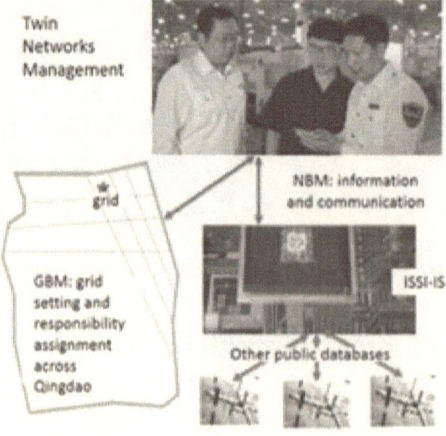

Since the GBM and NBM often work together like a pair as depicted below, they are widely known as Twin Networks Management (TNM).

B. Mobile Tool

The Mobile Tool was created in 2012 and, following a two-year pilot, was formally adopted in 2014. It is used through a mobile application (app) and a 4G mobile network. Inspectors and assistants can install the app on their smartphones, as illustrated below, and use it to collect, verify, transfer and analyse data available on the IDHRSS anytime, anywhere, quickly and accurately.

The Mobile Tool helps inspectors and assistants to connect with each other and with the Inspectorate and the IDHRSS. Through the tool, responsible inspectors and assistants receive alerts when the Inspectorate identifies a possible case of non-compliance among enterprises falling under their responsibility. This will then trigger a chain of actions, including an on-the-spot investigation and enforcement of compliance, as required.

This chain of actions proceeds quickly. For instance, an alert was issued in July 2015 concerning an enterprise suspected of non-compliance. Immediately, the responsible inspectors set off for the enterprise. Thanks to this on-the-spot inspection, the suspicion was confirmed. Of the enterprise's 265 workers, 98 did not have social insurance coverage. Enforcement measures were then put in place to ensure full compliance with the law.

To a certain extent, the Mobile Tool is seen as a mobile or advanced version of the TNM as it possesses enhanced and additional capacities, one of which is real-time filming and synchronic transmission. It is useful not only for data collection and transfer, but also for transparent dialogue and fairer inspection and enforcement.

C. Compliance Promotion Campaign (CPC)

To encourage employers and workers to comply with employment and social security laws in the first place, Qingdao has launched the Compliance Promotion Campaign. It has three interrelated elements.

- **Compliance appraisal** is carried out every two years to assess how well each enterprise has complied with employment and social security laws in the two preceding years. Based on the results, enterprises are classified into three categories, namely full, medium and poor compliance. The levels of compliance determine the level of inspections required for the following two years.

- **Compliance Medal** is awarded to those reaching the highest level of compliance in the category of full compliance. In 2014, a total of 581 enterprises received the Compliance Medal and had their names published in Qingdao Daily. After becoming medallists, routine inspection is waived for two years.

- **Public exposure** of enterprises and their worst cases of non-compliance generates social pressure that is expected to accelerate compliance among these enterprises. For instance, on 23 January 2014, the names of 21 non-compliant enterprises were released along with the arrears in paying salaries and social insurance contributions. On the following day, four of them paid the arrears. Furthermore, these enterprises face intensified inspection for the next two years.

This system is not unique to Qingdao, but exists all over the country. The practice of labour and social security inspection may vary slightly in different regions, but all have been critical in expanding social security coverage in the People's Republic of China.

5. References

Casale; Zhu. 2013. Labour administration reform in China (Geneva).

Labour and Social Security Bureau of Qingdao. 2013. 青岛市用人单位重大劳动保障违法行为社会公布办法 [Measure on disclosing publically severe law violations committed by working units] (Qingdao).

—. 2013. 青岛市劳动保障守法诚信示范用人单位评价办法 [Assessment measure on establishing a list of exemplary working units who have complied fully with employment and social security laws] (Qingdao).

—. 2013. 青岛市用人单位劳动保障守法诚信等级评价办法（试行）[Provisional measure on assessing and determining the degree of compliance of working units with the laws] (Qingdao).

Meng, Tong. 2015. 劳动保障监察对社保扩面的贡献 [Contributions of labour and social security inspection and enforcement of compliance to the extension of social protection coverage] (Beijing).

MOHRSS (Ministry of Human Resources and Social Security of the P.R.C); ILO. 2016. 中国劳动保险监察创新 [Innovation made in labor and social security inspection in China] (Beijing).

People's Congress of Qingdao. 2011. 青岛市劳动保险监察条例 [Labour and Social Security Inspection Regulation of Qingdao] (Qingdao).

People's Congress of Shandong Province. 2000. 山东省劳动保险监察条例 [Labour and Social Security Inspection Regulation of Shandong Province] (Jinan).

People's Congress of the People's Republic of China. 2010. 社会保险法 [Social Insurance Law] (Beijing).

QBS (Qingdao Bureau of Statistics). 2015. 2014年我市常住人口突破九百万 [The number of the regular residents in Qingdao exceeded 9 million in 2014] (Qingdao).

State Council. 2004. 劳动保险监察条例 [Labour and Social Security Inspection Regulation] (Beijing).

8

Colombia: System of Identification of Social Programme Beneficiaries[14]

A unified vulnerability assessment and identification system for social assistance: Through the establishment of a unified household vulnerability index, Colombia has channelled social assistance to those in need and reduced inequalities in the country.

The System of Identification of Social Programme Beneficiaries (SISBEN) produces a household vulnerability index that is used to identify the beneficiaries of social assistance programmes in Colombia. During the 1990s, the Government shifted public subsidies from the supply side of social and health services to the demand side, making it necessary to identify target groups that would receive subsidized social protection.

Progressively implemented since 1995, SISBEN is based on data collected by the country's 1,101 municipalities and districts. In 2013, ten institutions running several social protection and employment programmes were using SISBEN to identify potential beneficiaries.

In 2014, the SISBEN database held information on more than 34 million people, more than 70 per cent of the national population.

---

[14] This chapter was authored by Lucia Mina Rosero, Lina Castaño and Alfredo Sarmiento, with support from Thibault van Langenhove of the ILO and reviewed by Isabel Ortiz, Valérie Schmitt and Fabio Durán-Valverde of the ILO. It was first published in May 2015.

1. Main lessons learned

- A common system to assess vulnerabilities and identify potential beneficiaries can contribute to improve coherence across social protection programmes.
- It also helps improve the transparency and traceability of social protection system administration since entitlements are determined using a transparent methodology.
- By establishing one common mechanism to assess vulnerabilities and identify beneficiaries, social protection programmes were able to develop a more reliable identification system at a lower administrative cost.
- Local governments are invited to play an important role in collecting data that is used to develop and update SISBEN. The system has therefore fostered collaboration between national and local institutions.

2. The need for an identification tool in the context of shifting subsidies from supply to demand side

Colombia is the second most populated country in South America after Brazil. According to World Bank statistics, it counted 48.3 million inhabitants in 2013, of which 31 per cent live below the national poverty line. Income distribution is also unequal with a Gini coefficient of 53.5 in 2012, which ranks Colombia the 6th most unequal Latin American country.

Access to social protection is a constitutional right. Article 48 of the Constitution of Colombia (1991) states that "Social Security is a mandatory public service which will be delivered under the administration, coordination, and control of the State, subject to the principles of efficiency, universality, and cooperation within the limits established by law. All the population is guaranteed the irrevocable right to Social Security."

At the beginning of the 1990s, Colombia, like many other countries in the region, reformed its social protection system and shifted public subsidies from the supply of health and social services to the demand side (e.g. cash transfers, subsidies for social protection contributions, among others). At the onset, subsidies in the health sector were allocated to public and private health-promoting entities using existing municipalities' census lists and a socio-economic classification of households. These tools were inappropriate for identifying those most in need and contributed to the exclusion of a high proportion of people from social health protection.

In order to address this challenge, SISBEN was adopted to identify those most in need of protection, and based on each social protection programme's eligibility criteria, link the programme to a list of potential beneficiaries.

Figure 9: Logical flow for Colombia's SISBEN

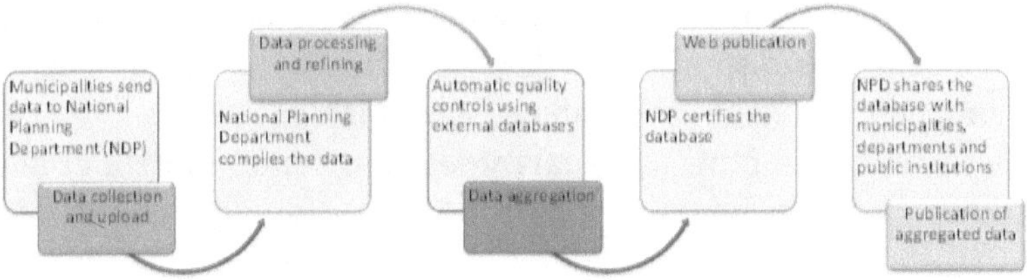

Source: Social CONPES (i.e. document approved by the National Council of Economic and Social Policy) 040 of September 1997.

3. An identification mechanism shared by ten institutions

SISBEN began operations in January 1995. In 1997 the National Planning Department (NPD) issued a rule instructing all municipalities and districts to adopt the system1. SISBEN has since become mandatory for all social programmes.

Since its creation, SISBEN has gone through three versions. The latest version (SISBEN-III) comprises three components: a socioeconomic survey to collect data, a welfare index to assess vulnerabilities, and software to estimate an index score for each household.

The SISBEN Welfare Index is defined by the NPD. Based on the Index, each household receives a score from 0 to 100 (from poorest to richest). The score is calculated by the software using 24 variables across four dimensions: health, education, housing, and vulnerability. Scores and variables are adjusted according to household location (main cities, urban areas, and rural areas). The vulnerability assessment takes into account two perspectives: 1) that of the individuals and households and 2) that of the context in which they live.

SISBEN is a nationally defined tool administered at the decentralized level. Municipalities/districts are responsible for the management of SISBEN in their territories through ad-hoc committees. Departmental coordinators liaise between NPD and municipalities/districts. The data collected at the local level is compiled in a national database, which is updated on a regular basis (every month). This guarantees consistency of data at any time and everywhere.

The collection of data is under the responsibility of municipalities and districts. They use two types of surveys: sweeping and on-demand. Sweeping surveys are similar to the census and are based on a door-to-door approach in the poorest geographical areas and neighbourhoods. The sweeping surveys are used to build the initial database and should be conducted every three years. People can update their data at any time through the on-demand survey when they need to correct names, add or remove household members, or to request a new assessment of their vulnerabilities.

Social programmes using SISBEN receive the national aggregated database from NPD. Based on their available budget and policy design, the programmes set the maximum eligibility score that will be applied and may choose additional eligibility criteria or qualifying conditions. By applying the score barrier, criteria, and conditions to the database, the SISBEN delivers a list of potential beneficiaries. In 2013, ten institutions running several social protection and employment programmes each used the SISBEN to identify potential beneficiaries: Ministry of Health and Social Protection, Ministry of Labour, Colombian Institute for Family Welfare (ICBF), National Ministry of Education, Department for Social Prosperity, Colombian Institute for Overseas Studies, Ministry of Agriculture, Ministry of Housing, Servicio Nacional de Aprendizaje, Registraduría Nacional del Estado Civil, and the Armed Forces.

4. This cost-effective mechanism channels social assistance to those in need and reduces inequalities

The use of a unified set of rules to assess vulnerability through the SISBEN has increased consistency and coherence across the social protection system in Colombia.

Additionally, existing programmes have saved administrative costs by sharing the burden of the development and maintenance of the SISBEN database. The average cost of a survey (sweeping and on-demand) is estimated at US$4.41 for SISBEN-II, which is lower than similar mechanisms adopted in Chile (US$10 in 2003) and Mexico (US$12 in 2000) (NPD, 2007). Conducting the national survey once every three years under SISBEN-II cost around 2 per cent of the annual cost of the subsidized health-care package.

SISBEN uses traceable and well-founded statistical techniques. It is coherent, decentralized, and embeds continuous monitoring and evaluation into its processes.

5. Next steps

Currently there are discussions about refining the definitions of individual and contextual vulnerabilities to better reflect Colombia's diversity. Households with identical conditions in terms of health, demographic structure, education, and assets have similar scores even though they may reside in areas with different availability and quality of public services. Indeed, these households should have different vulnerability levels, which is not yet the case under the current SISBEN.

Also, SISBEN does not fully capture transitory shocks, such as job loss, that may happen between sweeping surveys and are likely to have an impact on households' vulnerabilities. It might be necessary to establish complementary mechanisms to identify households affected by temporary contingencies.

SISBEN has the potential of being an effective tool for monitoring utilization of services and measuring the impact of social protection programmes on poverty and other dimensions. These functions still remain underdeveloped.

6. References

Azevedo, V.; Bouillon, CP.; Irarrázaval, I. 2011. La efectividad de las redes de protección social: El rol de los sistemas integrados de información social en seis países de América Latina (Washington, DC, Inter-American Development Bank (IDB)). Available at: http://www.iadb.org/es/publicaciones/detalle,7101.html?id=20 662.

Departamento Nacional de Planeación. 2007. "Mecanismos de focalización, cuatro estudios de caso", in Sistema de Indicadores Sociodemográficos para Columbia (SISD) Bulletin, No. 32.

—. 2008. Documento CONPES 117 DNP de 2008. (Bogotá). Available at:

www.icbf.gov.co/cargues/avance/docs/conpes_dnp_0117_2008
.htm.

—. 2009. Documentos Metodológicos. (Bogotá). Available at:
www.sisben.gov.co/Información/DocumentosMetodológicos.

—. 2015. SISBEN website. Available at: www.sisben.gov.co/.

Departamento Nacional de Planeación, Subdirección de
Promoción Social y Calidad de Vida. 2011. Guía para uso del
Sisbén III – Versión 2 (Bogotá).

Departamento Nacional de Planeación; Ministerio de Salud;
UNDP; Misión Social. 2001. Evaluación integral del SISBEN
(Bogotá).

Departamento Nacional de Planeación; UNDP; Misión Social.
2003. Quién se beneficia del Sisbén? Evaluación Integral
(Bogotá). Available at:
www.pnud.org.co/sitio.shtml?apc=a-c0200114--&x=18711.

Fresneda, O. 2003. "El sistema de selección de beneficiarios y el
régimen subsidiado de salud en Colombia", in Journal of
Comercio Exterior, Vol. 53, No. 6, pp. 574-586.

ILO. 2014. Colombia: Universalizing health protection (Geneva).
Available at:
www.social-
protection.org/gimi/gess/RessourcePDF.action?ressource.ressou
rceId=48019.

Lasso, F. 2006. Incidencia del gasto público social sobre la
distribución del ingreso y la reducción de la pobreza (Bogotá,
DNP, Misión para el diseño de una estrategia para la reducción
de la pobreza y la desigualdad (MERPD)).

Schmitt-Diabaté, V. 2008. "Colombia mission report" (Geneva,
ILO, Social Security Department). Available at: www.social-

protection.org/gimi/gess/ShowRessource.action?ressource.ress
ourceId=18538.

Velez, CE; Castaño, E; Deutsch, R. 1998. An economic
interpretation of Colombia's SISBEN: A composite welfare index
derived from the optimal scaling algorithm (Washington, DC,
Inter-American Development Bank IDB).

9

Ecuador: Financing social protection through debt restructuring[15]

Ecuador offers an excellent recent example of how restructuring sovereign debt can be used to create fiscal space for social development expenditures.

The idea of swapping debt for development has been around since the 1980s as a way out from the Latin American debt crisis. During the 1998-2008 decade, 18 debt swaps in 14 countries converted about US$608.8 million in debt into support for local development.

The Highly Indebted Poor Countries (HIPC) Initiative, launched in 1996 by the International Monetary Fund (IMF) and the World Bank, helped eligible countries reduce their debt service payments by about 1.8 per cent of gross domestic product (GDP) between 2001 and 2014. Linking debt relief to poverty reduction and social policies allowed these countries to increase their expenditures on health, education and other social services. On average, such spending is now about five times the amount of debt service payments.

However, only low-income countries could access HIPC. Other countries had to resort to debt restructuring. In recent years, more than 60 countries have successfully renegotiated and restructured debt, and directed debt servicing savings to

---

[15] This chapter was authored by Anis Chowdhury and reviewed by Isabel Ortiz, Jeronim Capaldo, Hiroshi Yamabana and Stefan Urban of the ILO. It was first published in August 2016.

development, including social programmes. It is now well accepted that countries can create fiscal space to increase social spending through debt restructuring linked to social programmes.

1. Main lessons learned

- Ecuador defaulted on its "illegitimate" debt and freed up public resources for expanding health care, education and social protection programmes. Social spending more than doubled from 4.8 per cent in 2006 to 10.3 per cent of GDP in 2011.
- The newly released public resources were also successfully used to help the economy recover from the 2008 financial crisis. GDP growth increased from 0.4 per cent in 2009 to 7.8 per cent in 2011, surpassing the pre-crisis growth rate of 7.2 per cent in 2008.
- Debt restructuring enabled the Government, through social and human development investments, to reduce poverty rates from 37.6 per cent in 2006 to 22.5 per cent in 2014, while the Gini coefficient (measuring inequality) declined from 0.54 to 0.47 during 2006-11.
- Contrary to critics' expectations, Ecuador's credit reputation did not suffer as its social investments are regarded as a developmental success. Ecuador was able to sell $2 billion worth of bonds in 2014 when it returned to the international capital markets.

2. Ecuador's default on "odious" debt expands fiscal space

In 2008, Ecuador held an official audit to assess the legitimacy of its sovereign foreign debt. The government-commissioned, two-year investigation concluded that some of its foreign debts violated multiple principles of international and domestic law and were therefore deemed "illegitimate". These were mostly private sector debts that had been nationalized by former Governments.

While Ecuador respected all the debt that had contributed to the country's development or the "legitimate" debt, it defaulted on two government bonds deemed "illegitimate", by suspending payments, during the depth of the global financial crisis in December 2008. Ecuador then bought them back at the going price of 35 cents on the dollar and retired them. This resulted in a significant reduction in interest payments as a percentage of GDP (Figure 10). The savings on principal and interest payments will amount to more than $7 billion over the period 2008-30. The freed up public resources were used for fiscal stimulus to cushion the impact of the 2008-09 global financial crisis and for expanding health care, education, social assistance and developing communications infrastructure.

Figure 10: Interest payments in Ecuador (% of GDP)

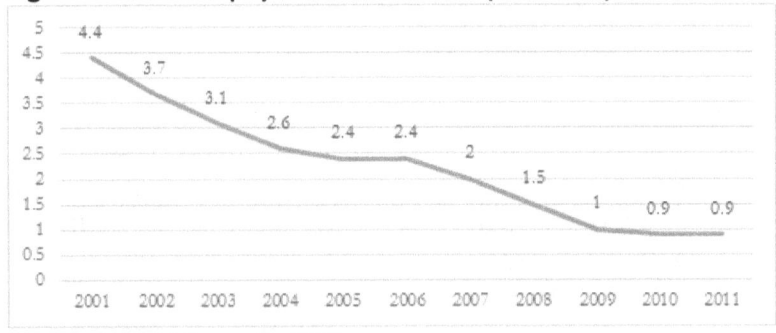

Source: Ray and Kozameh, 2012.

One of the elements of fiscal stimulus was expanded access to housing financing through Bono de la Vivienda programmes and concessional mortgage loans issued through Ecuador's Social Security Institute (IESS). The total housing loans in Ecuador grew by nearly 50 per cent in 2009, and IESS accounted for over half of all housing credit in 2011 (Figure 11). This contributed to a construction boom in early 2010 and helped the economy recover quickly from the recession. The overall GDP growth rate increased from 0.4 in 2009 to 7.8 per cent in 2011, surpassing the pre-crisis rate of 7.2 per cent in 2008 and catching up its 20-year growth trend.

Figure 11: Housing credit by source in Ecuador

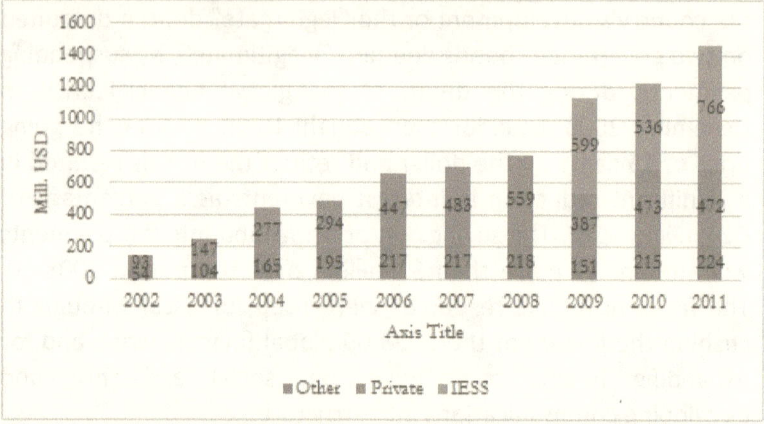

Note: IESS = Loans issued through the Social Security Institute.
Source: Ray and Kozameh, 2012.

3. Higher social spending

Public resources freed up in Ecuador through the debt write-down were invested in socio-economic development. Total social spending by the Central Government more than doubled from 4.8 per cent of GDP in 2006 to 10.3 per cent in 2011 (Figure 12). Government spending on education doubled from 2.6 to 5.2 per cent of GDP during the same period. Social welfare spending, which included housing assistance programmes for low-income families and the cash transfer, Bono de Desarrollo Humano (human development bond), also more than doubled from 0.7 to 1.8 per cent of GDP. This resulted in the expansion of Bono de Desarrollo Humano's coverage from 35.5 in 2005 to 44.3 per cent in 2010, the highest coverage rate among conditional cash transfer programmes in Latin America and the Caribbean.

Figure 12: Government social spending in Ecuador (% of GDP)

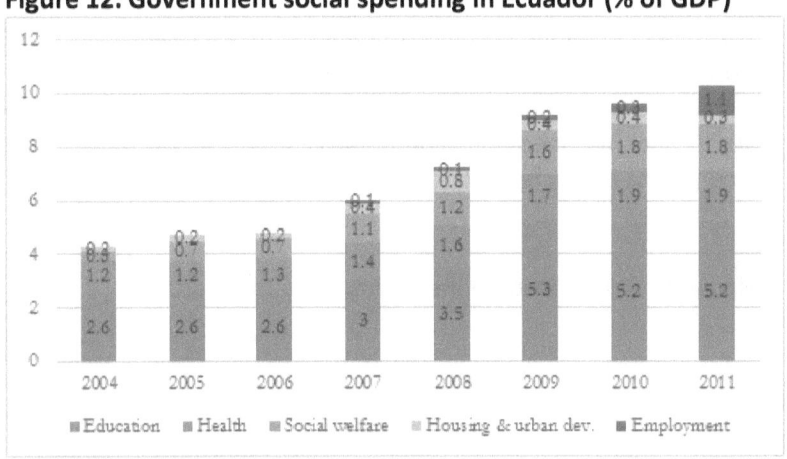

Source: Ray and Kozameh, 2012.

Figure 13: Poverty rate and Gini coefficient in Ecuador

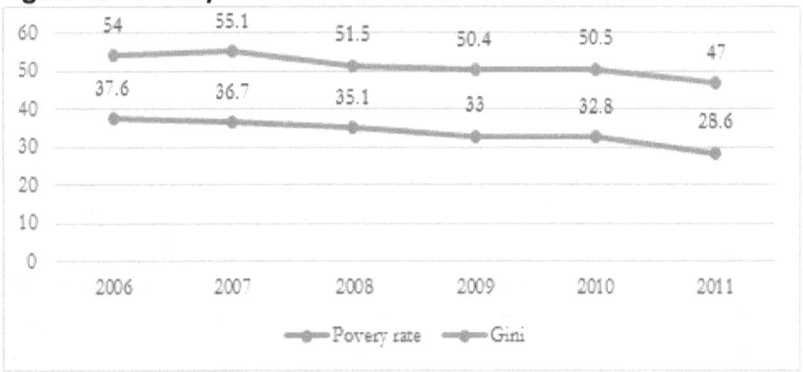

Source: Ray and Kozameh, 2012.

4. Human development accelerates

The results of increased public social spending on human development made possible by debt restructuring are impressive. For example, the national poverty rate dropped from 37.6 per cent in 2006 to 22.5 per cent in 2014 (Figure 13). This improvement is also reflected in the unemployment rate, which fell from 9.1 per cent in the 1st quarter of 2010 to 4.9 per cent in 2012.

The Gini coefficient, a common measure of inequality, declined from 0.54 to 0.47 during 2006-11 (Figure 13). The improvement in income distribution is also mirrored in the decline of the 90/10 income inequality ratio, which is the ratio between incomes of the richest 10 per cent and the poorest 10 per cent (Figure 14).

Figure 14: 90/10 income inequality ratio in Ecuador

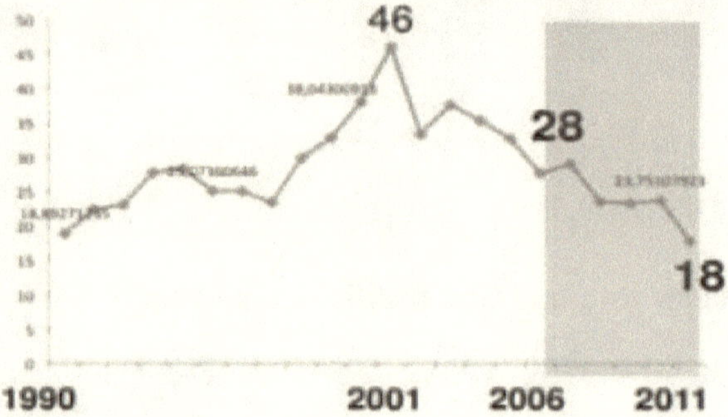

Source: Nehring, 2012.

The expansion of the Bono de Desarrollo Humano contributed to a sharp increase in the number of vaccinated children from 2.5 million in 2008 to 3.6 million in 2010. Between 2009 and 2015, 2,994,411 children under 5 years of age had preventive medical check-ups. More than 800,000 children received micro-nutrients and consumption of these nutrients has been monitored by children's centres. During this period, 6,571,169 children under 5 years of age with medical issues were treated and 3,078,408 prenatal examinations were performed with the provision of micro-nutrients. Thus, infant mortality declined from 20.7 (per 1,000 live births) in 2006 to 17.6 in 2010, and child mortality fell from 26.6 (per 1,000 children under age 5) to 23.0 during the same period. There have also been dramatic increases in pre-primary and secondary school enrolment rates (Figure 15).

By the end of 2015, Ecuador had achieved 20 of the 21 Millennium Development Goals, some beyond the standard minimum target.

Figure 15: School enrolment ratios (gross) in Ecuador

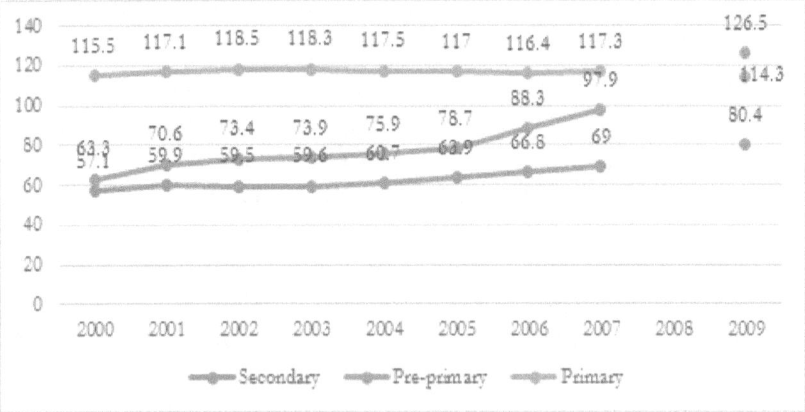

Source: Ray and Kozameh, 2012.

5. Conclusion

Ecuador suffered repeated debt crises after the early 1980s and public external debt remained high (over 66 per cent of GDP) in 2000. "Structural adjustment" packages of liberalization, privatization and labour market reforms failed to reignite growth on a sustained basis while the country's social and human conditions deteriorated significantly with more than 60 per cent of its population living in poverty in the late 1990s. Ecuador's human development index (HDI) was 0.6 in 1980, which improved only marginally to 0.674 in two decades.

However, Ecuador's socio-economic development since the beginning of the new millennium has been impressive. Ecuador's HDI value for 2014 was 0.732, putting the country in the high human development category. Its social development accelerated since 2009 when it expanded its fiscal space by writing down its external debts that were deemed "illegitimate" in order to strengthen its social protection and increase social spending. Perhaps this explains why Ecuador's credit reputation was not permanently damaged contrary to the general perception. It was able to sell $2 billion in bonds in June 2014 at its first return to the international capital market. Thus, Ecuador offers lessons for other developing countries on how to successfully restructure external debt for social development. Based on the experience of Ecuador, as well as Norway, a special United Nations Commission of Experts on Reforms of the International Monetary and Financial System came out in support of public debt audits as a mechanism for transparent and fair restructuring of debts. Debt audits are ongoing in several other countries, including Bolivia, Brazil, Greece, Ireland and the Philippines.

Debt management is one of the eight alternatives that countries have to expand fiscal space for social protection. Governments normally use a mix of taxes and social security contributions to fund social protection, combined with other options (Ortiz et al, 2015).

6. References

Buckley, R. 2009. "Debt-for-development exchanges: The origins of a financial technique", in The Law and Development Review, Vol. 2, No. 1, pp. 24-49.

European Report on Development. 2014. European Report on Development 2015: Financing and other means of implementation in the post-2015 context, Ecuador country illustration. Available at: https://ec.europa.eu/europeaid/sites/devco/files/erd5-country-illustration-ecuador-2015_en.pdf.

Fattorelli, M.L. 2014. Citizen public debt audit: Experiences and methods (Liège, CADTM and Geneva, CETIM).

IMF. 2016. Debt Relief under the heavily indebted poor countries (HIPC) initiative – Factsheet (Washington, DC).

Available   at:
https://www.imf.org/external/np/exr/facts/hipc.htm.

Krugman, P. 1989. Market-based debt-reduction schemes, NBER Working Paper No. 1323. (Cambridge, Mass., National Bureau for Economic Research).

Nehring, R. 2012. Social protection in Ecuador: A new vision for inclusive growth, International Policy Research Brief, No. 28, August 2012, (Brasilia, International Policy Centre for Inclusive Growth).

Ortiz, I.; Cummins, M.; Karunanethy, K. 2015. Fiscal space for social protection: Options to expand social investments in 187 Countries, ESS Working Paper No. 48 (Geneva, International Labour Office).

Ray, R.; Kozameh, S. 2012. Ecuador's economy since 2007 (Washington, DC, Center for Economic and Policy Research).

Salmon, F. 2009. Lessons from Ecuador's bond default. Available at: http://blogs.reuters.com/felix-salmon/2009/05/29/lessons-from-ecuadors-bond-default/

10

India: Worker Facilitation Centres[16]

In a country with a vast informal economy and limited awareness of and access to social protection, Worker Facilitation Centres (WFCs) follow a proactive approach to reach out to people in remote areas.

The WFC is a single-window service available to informal economy households in the State of Karnataka in India. The centres improve access to social protection benefits by acting as a crucial bridge between government departments operating social protection schemes and informal economy households.

WFCs believe in taking social protection to the households of the beneficiaries instead of waiting for them to approach the centres. Their primary functions include, among others:

- identifying and recording information on eligible households and members;
- assisting people with the documentation required to register for schemes and claim benefits; and
- providing information on and creating awareness of social protection.[17]

---

[16] This chapter was authored by Hans-Christoph Ammon and Namerta Sharma of GIZ, D Rajasekhar of the Institute for Social and Economic Change, and Loveleen De and Jurriaan Linsen of the ILO and reviewed by Isabel Ortiz and Valérie Schmitt of the ILO. It was first published in August 2015.

[17] In September 2015, the Government of Karnataka launched Single Window Service Centres (SWSCs) that provide the same functions as the WFCs as well as employment services.

1. Main lessons learned

- WFCs are a concrete mechanism to implement the provisions of the Unorganised Workers' Social Security Act of 2008.
- WFCs show how a single window and case management can help households to access social protection services and benefits by facilitating complex procedural requirements and addressing the drawbacks of a fragmented delivery system.
- Community Facilitators (CFs) or other people who work at the WFCs visit beneficiary households to inform remote and vulnerable population groups about their right to social protection and include them in existing social protection schemes. The proactive approach followed by WFCs can be an inspiration for countries with many social protection schemes and low coverage.
- A well-designed management information system (MIS) bridges the gap between the Government's existing programmes and intended beneficiaries. In addition, strict quality control systematically monitors CFs and contributes to the effectiveness and efficiency of the delivery mechanism.

2. Why is there a need for WFCs?

In India, 93 per cent of the workforce is in the informal or unorganized sector, which contributes around 60 per cent of the gross domestic product (GDP). Informal sector workers usually do not have a direct, formal or contractual relationship with their employers; therefore, they lack access to sufficient and reliable social security benefits. On the demand side, there are intrinsic challenges, such as illiteracy among workers, low awareness of entitlements and a lack of access to organizations or groups that can represent workers' interests. On the supply side, social policies are fragmented with low convergence among schemes, information management is inadequate and transaction costs are high.

In 2008, the Government of India passed the Unorganised Workers' Social Security Act, which stipulates minimum social security measures for informal sector workers, including health and maternity benefits, old-age pensions and death and disability grants. Subsequently, national- and state-level social security boards were set up to implement the provisions of the Act. The Act also encourages the formation of WFCs.

Recognizing the need to bridge the gap between the Government's existing programmes and intended beneficiaries, the Department of Labour of Karnataka, with support from the German International Cooperation (GIZ), set up Worker Facilitation Centres in 2011. The main objectives of WFCs are to provide information on social protection schemes, identify and register prospective beneficiaries, and help the users to access benefits and services.

WFCs are set up at the lowest administrative levels of government, i.e. village councils or urban wards. Each WFC covers 1,000 households, including in remote areas. Thus, they reduce the high opportunity costs for informal sector beneficiaries to access services.

3. How do WFCs function?

WFCs cover informal economy workers, such as agricultural labourers, construction workers, domestic helpers, garment workers and home-based workers in Karnataka. These workers rarely have formal labour contracts, access to social protection or entitlements to the minimum wage.

There are 250 WFCs in Karnataka, housed in village council offices (in rural areas) or municipal offices (in urban areas). The Centres are equipped with computers, printers and Internet access, and are run by Community Facilitators from the same locality. This contributes to their acceptability by beneficiaries. CFs conduct household visits to perform several functions:

- identify eligible beneficiary households and collect basic household information;
- upload the information on an MIS;
- disseminate information on existing social protection schemes for the unemployed, sick, injured, elderly and survivors, as well as on education scholarships;
- assist beneficiaries to obtain, fill and submit the necessary documents and application forms; and
- follow up on benefit claims.

Figure 16: Institutional framework of the WFCs in India

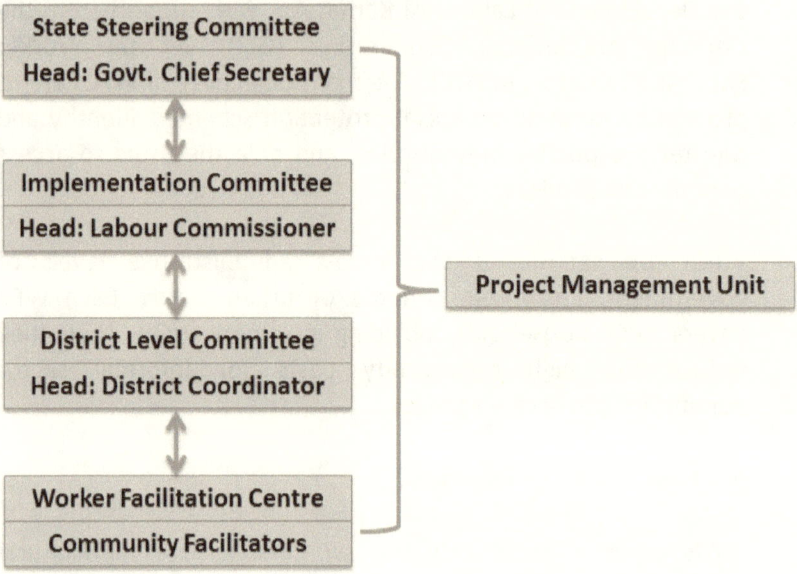

Source: GIZ.

CFs play a special role as they do not wait for beneficiaries to come to the centres and apply for benefits. Instead, CFs visit the households within the WFC's jurisdiction. To ensure alignment between their work and the State's agenda on social protection delivery, the WFCs have governing committees at different levels of government (see Figure 16).

The State Steering Committee, headed by the Chief Secretary of the Government, provides overall guidance for inter-departmental coordination and cooperation. The Implementation Committee, headed by the Commissioner of Labour, discusses the problems related to the implementation of the project and takes corrective actions. The District Coordination Committee facilitates inter-departmental cooperation for convergence of different benefits and greater outreach towards beneficiaries. The WFCs are at the lowest level of this institutional framework. They are overseen by a Project Management Unit consisting of technical staff and the State Coordinator. The Project Management Unit interacts with all levels to analyse, consolidate and share information, and coordinate quality checks and impact studies.

All this information along with data on prospective beneficiaries, existing social protection schemes and data from other relevant government departments, are consolidated in a custom-designed MIS. Data on beneficiaries are collected by CFs through surveys and updated into beneficiary database. The quality of these surveys is monitored by a third party that samples and conducts reverse checks on the surveys.

The Community Facilitators undergo capacity training for their role. The training covers a conceptual understanding of social protection, key social protection schemes, conditions of informal economy workers and communication skills.

4. What impact have WFCs had so far?

The social protection system in India is affected by many challenges that create barriers to access, such as inadequate and poorly disseminated information, a complex delivery system and high illiteracy and poverty rates. Against this backdrop, WFCs have helped to identify and register eligible households and facilitate their access to benefits. WFCs have also significantly improved coverage of schemes that are most relevant to informal economy workers, including health and accident insurance, death benefits and pensions.

The MIS used by the WFCs contains data on 260,348 households out of a total estimated 361,525 informal economy households in Karnataka. Of these households, 260,470 individuals were found to be eligible for existing social protection schemes. Community Facilitators have helped to submit applications for 47 per cent of these eligible individuals. Of these applications to existing schemes, 72 per cent have been approved.

Findings of a randomized controlled trial conducted in 2012 show that WFCs have helped increase people's awareness of social protection schemes and improved access to them. For instance, the coverage of Rashtriya Swasthya Bima Yojna (National Health Insurance Scheme) was 75 per cent higher in households covered by WFCs. The study also showed that older Centres performed better, which suggests that the performance of WFCs improves over time.

5. What's next?

Certain bottlenecks hamper the effective coverage of all eligible beneficiaries:

- Slightly over 50 per cent of eligible individuals have not yet had their applications submitted.
- Submitting applications involves complex and time-consuming procedures, such as filling separate forms for different schemes and providing formal documents, such as proof of age, which are difficult for informal economy members to acquire.
- Informal economy households are often reluctant to register for contributory schemes as they may not understand the mechanisms and advantages of insurance and may not have clear information about the benefits they would receive in future.

To address these bottlenecks and increase the effectiveness of the centres, the Government of Karnataka decided to expand the WFC model in September 2015. This was done by launching 1,200 Single Window Service Centres that provide training and employment services in addition to WFC functions.

6. References

Berg, E.; Rajasekhar, D.; Manjula, R. 2014. Social security benefits for unorganised workers in Karnataka: Programme evaluation report (Bangalore, Deutsche Gesellschaft für Internationale Zusammenarbeit).

GIZ. Single Window Service Karnataka, project website. Available at: http://sws-karnataka.org/.

Nagaraj, R. 2012. Growth, inequality and social development in India: Is inclusive growth possible? (Hampshire, United Nations Research Institute for Social Development and Palgrave Macmillan).

National Commission for Enterprises in the Unorganized Sector (NCEUS). 2007. Report on conditions of work and promotion of livelihoods in the unorganised sector (New Delhi). Available at: www.nceuis.nic.in [15 July 2015].

—. 2006. Social security for unorganised workers (New Delhi). Available at: www.nceuis.nic.in [15 July 2015].

Rajasekhar, D.; Suchitra, J.Y.; Madheswaran, S.; Karanth, G.K. 2006. Design and management of social security benefits for unorganised sector workers in Karnataka (New Delhi, Deutsche Gesellschaft für Internationale Zusammenarbeit).

Sen, G.; Rajasekhar, D. 2012. Social protection policies, experiences and challenges (New York, Palgrave Macmillan).

11

India: Rashtriya Swasthya Bima Yojna[18]

By effectively integrating technology into the design of its scheme, RSBY has significantly extended health protection to vulnerable and informal workers and is becoming one of the main platforms to deliver social protection.

When it was launched on 1 April 2008, RSBY had two main objectives:

- to increase access for informal economy workers to quality health care
- to reduce out-of-pocket expenditures on hospitalization

RSBY is now implemented in 28 states and union territories of India. As of April 2014, 37.2 million families are enrolled in the scheme and around 7.16 million hospitalization cases have benefitted from the scheme. Initially targeted at the Below Poverty Line (BPL) population, the programme now covers more categories of unorganized workers.

RSBY's information technology (IT) platform is now successfully used to administer other social security schemes. These standardization efforts could lead to greater efficiency and transparency of social security schemes in India.

---

[18] This chapter was authored by Thibault van Langenhove and Loveleen De of the ILO and reviewed by Isabel Ortiz, Valérie Schmitt, Markus Rück and Xenia Scheil-Adlung of the ILO. It was first published in September 2015.

1. Main lessons learned

- Social health protection schemes should be user-friendly with beneficiaries at their centre. RSBY—a paperless, cashless, and portable scheme—is adapted to its beneficiaries who are primarily poor, often illiterate, and largely migrant.
- A comprehensive communication strategy with customized messages for target groups should be prepared at the start of any social health protection scheme. Being aware that poor families often have little or no knowledge about insurance, particular emphasis should be placed on making the beneficiaries aware of the scheme, its benefits, and their eligibility.
- A national social protection scheme can function smoothly only if there is a certain degree of standardization in terms of the tools and technology being used across the country. At the same time, the technology used should be adapted to the conditions on the ground.
- Advanced technology, such as the use of smart cards, can contribute to expanding coverage and give access to health-care services for populations that are illiterate and without identity documents.

2. An affordable health insurance that provides financial protection to the poor, unorganized workers, and their families

Health care in India is financed through various sources, including individual out-of-pocket payments, central and state government tax revenues, private companies' initiatives, social contributions, and external aid. National Health Accounts data from 2004-05 show that combined expenditures of central, state, and local governments accounted for only about 20 per cent of total health expenditures in India while households accounted for nearly 60 per cent.

To reduce out-of-pocket expenditures and extend health coverage to the uncovered, the federal Government launched the Rashtriya Swasthya Bima Yojana (RSBY) on 1 April 2008 under the responsibility of the Central Ministry of Labour and Employment (MoLE). The objectives of RSBY are to reduce financial barriers to access hospital care and eliminate catastrophic health-care costs for the poor population, some categories of unorganized workers, and their families. In addition, the programme is tasked with improving the availability of health services and service delivery, as well as empowering beneficiaries by giving them a choice to select the empanelled hospitals where they wish to seek treatment.

RSBY is structured as a public-private partnership. It is led by the central Government, but implemented by authorities in India's states and union territories in cooperation with insurance companies, hospitals (public and private), and civil society organizations.

The scheme is financed from states' and the central Government's budgets and operated by insurance companies that are selected in each state through an open bidding process. The premium for the scheme is shared between the central Government and state governments at a ratio of 75:25, and 90:10 for north-eastern states. Additionally, the central Government bears the cost of the membership cards at a rate of 60 Indian rupees (INR) per card.

INR30 registration fees are collected at the state level and used to cover administrative costs. The overall cost incurred for issuing a card (including its production cost of about INR30, awareness activities carried out by the insurer for enrolment, the cost of the hardware to print the card, human resource training, among other costs) varies between INR75-100 depending on the location where the membership card is issued.

RSBY had to answer to the constraints and characteristics of its beneficiary group. First, it was clear from the outset that since the targeted beneficiaries are poor, they could not be expected to pay cash up-front and receive reimbursement later. Therefore, the scheme had to be cashless. Second, the beneficiaries are mostly illiterate and unable to read documents. The scheme, therefore, needed to be paperless. Third, some of the target population are migratory in nature, making it necessary for beneficiaries to access benefits across many locations. Thus, the scheme needed to be portable across India.

3. An insurance scheme that is cashless, paperless, and portable

RSBY aims to cover the entire BPL population—estimated to be approximately 70 million families comprising 350 million persons—and many categories of unorganized workers by 2017. The BPL families are identified through household surveys conducted by state administrations, while various government departments prepare lists of unorganized workers. Starting in 2011, eligibility for RSBY was extended to new categories of informal workers, including street vendors, domestic workers, rag-pickers, taxi and rickshaw drivers, and mine workers.

RSBY provides insurance coverage for selected hospitalization expenses and outpatient procedures up to INR30,000 (approximately US$500) per annum for a family with a maximum of five members on a floater basis.[19] Transportation charges are covered up to a ceiling of INR1,000 per year with a limit of INR100 per hospitalization. In addition to the hospitalization itself, insurance coverage starts up to one day prior to hospitalization, covering tests and medication leading up to the hospitalization. The insurance also covers medicines and other assistance required by the patients up to five days after the date

---

[19] Floater basis means that total amount can be used by one person or jointly with other members of the family.

of discharge from the hospital. RSBY covers all pre-existing diseases from day one and does not have an age limit.

In order to be cashless, paperless, and portable, the scheme relies on the use of membership cards. Each family pays a fee of INR30 to join the scheme and provides the first and last names of the household head, spouse, and up to three other designated beneficiaries. All family members enrolling in the scheme must be present on the day of enrolment to be photographed and fingerprinted. Using a laptop, scanner, and card printer, the registration team generates an RSBY membership card on the spot. Insurance company representatives provide the families with information about their benefits and a list of empanelled hospitals where they can receive services. Beneficiaries under RSBY can seek treatment at any one of the 10,000 public or private empanelled hospitals. Upon admission, the hospital verifies the patient's identify by checking their fingerprint. If the fingerprint matches one of the prints stored on the card and sufficient funds from the INR30,000 annual allowance remain on the family card, the patient receives cashless treatment.

The development of this genuine identification system based on a membership card was necessary in a country that lacks a national civil database and identity papers covering the whole population. A government officer is always present at the enrolment station in order to verify the identities of potential beneficiaries and make sure they meet the eligibility criteria. After delivering services, the hospital uses the RSBY-specific transaction software, which records all information on card bearers, the care they received, and the costs involved, to send a paperless claim to the insurance company and a record to the state and central governments. After reviewing the claims, the insurance company settles them directly through online transactions with the hospital.

4. **The scheme is successful in improving effective access to health care**

Access to health care among the RSBY beneficiary population has improved considerably in the past five years. According to an internal evaluation survey, hospitalization rates in RSBY districts have increased to three time those found in the National Sample Survey data for the poorest 40 per cent of the population (5.04 per cent versus 1.75 per cent). Additionally, 90 per cent of the beneficiaries who have received treatment under RBSY are satisfied with the treatment and services provided the hospitals.

One of the objectives of RSBY was to minimize out-of-pocket payments. A survey carried out in the states of Jharkhand, Maharashtra, and Punjab shows that while 90 per cent of the RSBY enrolled patients did not spend anything upon treatment, poor patients who were eligible but not enrolled in RSBY spent on average INR17,000 per year for hospitalization (Ghosh, 2012). However, another evaluation from Gujarat concluded that "nearly 60 per cent of insured patients had to spend about 10 per cent of their annual income on hospital expenses, despite being enrolled" (Narayanan et al., 2013). Access to health services is also limited by the annual ceiling of INR30,000 per family, which may prove too little for major surgeries. However, this ceiling may be raised to INR50,000 in the coming years.

Due to an unequal distribution of the health workforce and infrastructure in India, many people, especially in rural areas, lack access to health care. According to internal surveys, RSBY is creating demand for health services in rural areas, which has in turn created an incentive for private players to set up hospitals. It is of interest to further document the required conditions (notably in terms of regulation) for these private initiatives to result in increasing effective access to health care for vulnerable populations without increasing inequities.

5. What's next?

RSBY is gradually demonstrating that it is not only able to effectively deliver health insurance to poor and vulnerable sections of society, but has also created an IT platform which can deliver other social security benefits.

Other ministries and departments have expressed interest in using the RSBY platform to deliver their social security schemes. The Department of Financial Services has decided to use the RSBY platform to deliver a life and disability insurance called Aam Aadmi Bima Yojana. The Ministry of Rural Development has decided to deliver the National Social Assistance Programme (which also targets BPL) through the RSBY platform.

Learning from RSBY will help the Government of India to develop an effective model to achieve its goal of universal health coverage. Areas which may require further attention include: (1) extending coverage to all informal economy workers, (2) revising the benefits package to reflect increasing costs of treatment, as well as out-patient and tertiary care services, (3) strengthening existing systems for identifying fraud and addressing grievances, and (4) improving the quality of health services provided under RSBY.

6. References

Ghosh, R. 2012. Evaluation study of Rashtriya Swasthya Bima Yojana, A study of Jharkhand, Maharashtra and Punjab (NOIDA, V V Giri National Labour Institute).

GIZ. 2011. Health insurance for India's poor (Eschborn). Available at: http://health.bmz.de/good-practices/GHPC/Health_Insurance_India/RSBY_EN_long.pdf

Ministry of Labour and Employment, Government of India. 2014. Rashtriya Swasthya Bima Yojana (RSBY) operational manual (New Delhi). Available at:

www.rsby.gov.in/Documents.aspx?ID=2.

Narayanan, D.; Seshadri, T.; Trivedi, M.; Criel, B. 2013. "Promoting universal financial protection: Evidence from the Rashtriya Swasthya Bima Yojana (RSBY) in Gujarat, India" Health Research Policy and Systems, Vol. 11, No. 29.

National Health Accounts Cell, Ministry of Health and Family Welfare. 2009. National Health Accounts, 2004-05 (New Delhi). Available at: www.planningcommission.nic.in/reports/genrep/health/National_Health_Account_04_05.pdf.

Rao, G.; Choudhury, M. 2012. Health care financing reforms in India, National Institute of Public Finance and Policy Working Paper No: 2012-100 (New Delhi, National Institute of Public Finance and Policy).

Rathi, P.; Mukherji, A.; Sen, G. 2012. "Rashtriya Swasthya Bima Yojana: Evaluating utilisation, roll-out and perceptions in Amaravati District, Maharashtra", in Economic and Political Weekly, Vol. 47, No. 39, pp. 57-64.

RSBY, Monitoring and Evaluation. 2014. RSBY final draft report (Delhi). Available at: www.rsby.gov.in/Documents.aspx?ID=2.

Scheil-Adlung, X. 2014. Universal Health Protection: Progress to date and the way forward, Social Protection Policy Papers, Paper 10 (Geneva, ILO).

Seshadri, T.; Trivedi, M.; Saxena, D.; Nair, R.; Soors, W.; Criel, B.; Devadasan, N. 2011. Study of Rashtriya Swasthya Bima Yojana (RSBY) Health Insurance in India (Bangalore, Institute of Public Health). Available at: www.iphindia.org/v2/wp-content/uploads/2013/01/RSBY-report_2013_Jan_02.pdf.

12

Indonesia: Financing social protection through contributions and the removal of fuel subsidies[20]

Indonesia reprioritized its spending by cutting expensive fuel subsidies and successfully managing the political resistance by putting in place a compensatory scheme supporting low-income families. In parallel, the Government extended social protection by supporting the creation of a universal health-care system and extending pension coverage.

In the wake of the Asian Financial Crisis in 1997-98, the Government of Indonesia provided targeted safety nets but soon realized that they were inadequate. Indonesia endeavoured to extend social protection coverage to the entire population. A 2002 amendment to Indonesia's 1945 Constitution recognizes the right to social security for all and the responsibility of the State in the development of social security. Indonesia has committed to achieving universal health coverage by 2019 through a coordinated approach of contributory and non-contributory schemes.

The subsequent sections highlight how the Government of Indonesia is achieving universality and progressive implementation of the right to social protection. It will also discuss how Indonesia tackled the problem of unsustainable fuel subsidies by introducing cash transfers to offset the adverse impact on the poor.

---

[20] This chapter was authored by Anis Chowdhury and reviewed by Isabel Ortiz, Jeronim Capaldo, Hiroshi Yamabana and Stefan Urban of the ILO. It was first published in August 2016.

1. Main lessons learned

- Indonesia recognizes social protection as a constitutional right to its citizens.
- The Government gradually withdrew the fuel subsidy policy while concurrently extending social services, including educational assistance, health care and conditional cash transfers.
- Gradually, the Government built capacities to extend health care to the entire population, creating a universal health-care system (Jaminan Kesehatan Nasional (JKN)), which is consistent with the ILO Social Protection Recommendation, No. 202 (2012). The contribution-financed scheme now covers 145 million members, where contributions for the poor and near-poor are covered by the Government.
- The Government successfully extended health-care coverage to the informal sector and is now covering both public and private sector workers under the newly designed pension scheme.

2. Social protection system in Indonesia

Social protection in Indonesia is a shared responsibility between all stakeholders – the State, employers, workers, families and communities. Extended family and community support still plays a large role while a constitutionally mandated formal structure is taking shape. Indonesia now has a three-pillar social security system, namely:

- social assistance and services that are funded by the State. Beneficiaries include older persons, the poor, schools and micro-business;
- a public pension funded through compulsory contributions into a provident fund; and

- social insurance funded by compulsory contributions by workers, while the Government pays premiums for the poor.

From July 2015, five social security schemes are operational in Indonesia, namely:

1. occupational accident scheme: contribution of between 0.24 per cent and 1.74 per cent, depending on the type of business, paid by employers;
2. death benefit: contribution of 0.3 per cent, paid by employers;
3. old-age benefit scheme: contribution of 5.7 per cent (3.7 per cent paid by employers, 2 per cent by employees);
4. health-care protection scheme: contribution of 5 per cent (4 per cent paid by employers, 1 per cent paid by employees). Informal sector workers and non-employee: between 25,000 and 59,500 Indonesian rupiahs (IDR) per person per month, depending on the choice of class of facilities; and
5. pension scheme: contribution of 3 per cent (1 per cent paid by the employee, 2 per cent by the employer). In addition, permanent employees are entitled to severance pay: 1 month salary (<1 year working period), and up to 9 months' salary (>8 years working period).

There are three important milestones in the development of social security in Indonesia. First, the early recognition of social protection as a right, as stated in the 1945 Constitution of Indonesia. Second, in the mid-1960s, the Government gradually developed social security schemes, but limited them to formal sector workers. Third, driven by the effects of the Asian Financial Crisis (AFC) at the end of the 1990s, the Governments established a stronger social security system by adopting universal coverage.

The post AFC era was characterized by ad hoc and targeted programmes, leaving a large proportion of the poor uncovered, while there was substantial benefit leakage to the non-poor. Programmes included: a rice subsidy; school scholarships and block grants; health card for the poor with free access to public health services; a labour-intensive work programme; and the provision of grants to selected community groups.

As a result of the rather poor outcomes of these targeted programmes, the Government adopted the principle of universal coverage by amending the 1945 Constitution in 2002. An important step was the passing of the Law regarding the National Social Security System (SJSM) in 2004. The Law stipulates five social insurance programmes: (i) pension; (ii) old-age savings; (iii) health-related benefits; (iv) work accident compensation; and (v) death grants. It provides a framework for integrating various existing social security schemes with new schemes, as well as the expansion of social security coverage to the entire population.

The Law follows a staircase approach with non-contributory schemes for the poor, contributory schemes for the self-employed, and statutory social security schemes for formal sector workers. Universal health insurance under the Law on Health Social Security Providers (BPJS Kesehatan (BPJS I)) commenced in 2014, while other schemes, under Law No. 24/2011 on Social Security Providers (BPJS Ketenagakerjaan (BPJS II)), started in 2015. On the social assistance front, efforts to extend coverage to reach the poorest and most vulnerable and to better coordinate programmes are in progress.

During this phase, Indonesia also had to deal with the Global Financial Crisis (GFC). Indonesia responded with a fiscal stimulus package which contained expanded social protection measures. About 7 per cent of the stimulus package announced during 2008-09 was targeted at social protection.

3. Indonesia's fuel subsidy reforms and expansion of social protection

Indonesia's universal oil subsidy was initiated in 1967 to distribute the state's oil windfall to ordinary citizens. Ironically,

Indonesia became a net oil importer in 2004 when international oil prices were soaring, putting pressure on the national budget. Thus, Indonesia had no choice but to reform its fuel subsidy system.

Reducing the fuel subsidy in 2005 led to an increase in prices by 30 and 114 per cent in March and October 2005, respectively. When rioting broke out in 2005, the Government responded quickly by introducing a compensation programme for the poor consisting of educational assistance, health care and unconditional cash transfers (UCTs). The UCTs consisted of a cash benefit of IDR100,000 (roughly $10.50) per month to each target household, covering 15.5 million households or nearly a quarter of the population. The programme was not financially sustainable however and in 2006, the Government prepared to switch to conditional cash transfers (CCTs) through the Hopeful Family Programme.

Figure 17: Fuel subsidies as a share of central government expenditure in Indonesia, 2002–11

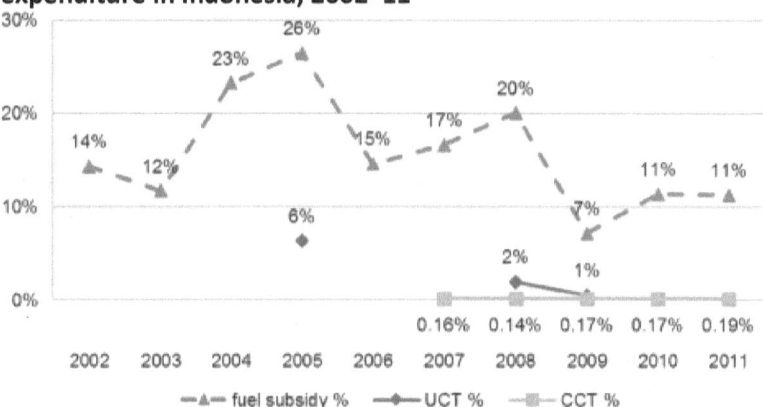

Source: Huck-ju Kwon and Woo-rim Kim, 2015.

The UCT was primarily introduced in the context of fiscal consolidation at the time of the economic crisis. As can be seen from Figure 17, UCTs and CCTs consistently made up a small share of government expenditures, while fuel subsidies were cut substantial. Its share in government expenditures dropped from

26 per cent in 2005 to 11 per cent in 2010-11, while expenditures on CCTs remained low. This represents a lost opportunity to further expand social protection through savings from fuel subsidies.

4. Towards universal health coverage

The first social health programme targeting poor households started in 1994 with the Health-card Programme. The programme changed its name in 2005 to Health Insurance for Poor Households (Asuransi Kesehatan bagi Keluarga Miskin or ASKESKIN) and initiated the first phase moving towards universal health coverage. Initially targeted to poor households, ASKESKIN evolved into the Health Security for Society (Jaminan Kesehatan Masyarakat or JAMKESMAS) programme in 2008, aiming at universal health coverage through a mandatory public health insurance programme.

The programme accounted for about 7 per cent of Indonesia's total social protection spending in 2009 and sought to reach 76.4 million people, or about one third of the total population. The cost to the Government per insured individual amounted to IDR6,250 (roughly $0.7).

In 2014, the Government launched a national health insurance scheme, Jaminan Kesehatan Nasional (JKN), to provide insurance to the entire population. BPJS Kesehatan has been established to implement the scheme. JKN is a unified, contribution-financed health insurance scheme and has 145 million members. The contributions for the poor and near-poor are paid by the Government.

In 2014, 86.4 million people were eligible for contribution assistance (PBI). The Government spent IDR19.9 trillion ($1.43 billion) financing PBI, more than double the 2013 budget allocation. However, it amounted to only IDR19,225 ($1.4) per person per month, significantly lower than actuarial estimates of a sustainable premium. Despite remarkable progress in the first year, many doubt whether JKN's budget will be sufficient to cover the unlimited and comprehensive service benefits.

5. Challenges

Successive Governments' political commitments are not matched by budgetary allocations. For example, only 2.2 per cent of the total government budget is allocated for health. In addition, there are supply-side and administrative challenges. Indonesia has critical shortages of health workers, hospitals and clinics for a nation with more than 250 million people.

Implementing a universal social protection system across more than 17,000 islands with a decentralized administration spanning 34 provinces and around 500 districts poses serious administrative challenges. Health issues (including finance and infrastructure) have been designated as the district government's responsibility. However, the role of local governments remains unclear in the grand design of universal health coverage. More encouragingly, universal health-care coverage is playing an import role in local electoral politics. This is creating pressure on local politicians to give priority to social protection and to adopt participatory budgeting.

6. Conclusion

Indonesia offers some interesting lessons. It has set an example by recognizing social protection as a constitutional right of its citizens. It took politically bold steps to reprioritize its spending by cutting expensive fuel subsidies and putting in place various compensatory schemes to attenuate the negative impact from the subsidy cuts on low-income families. Indonesia missed an opportunity to finance much of its social protection programmes with the funds freed from the fuel subsidy. Yet, it is still expanding its social protection system through contribution collection, subsidizing only those that cannot afford to pay, thus building a stronger base for the extension of coverage and services.

Removing fuel subsidies and expanding contributory revenues are two of the many alternatives that countries have to expand fiscal space for social protection. Other options are explained in the paper, "Fiscal space for social protection: Options to expand social investments in 187 countries".

7. References

Beaton, C.; Lontoh, L. 2010. Lessons learned from Indonesia`s attempts to reform fossil-fuel subsidies (Winnipeg, International Institute for Sustainable Development). Available at: www.iisd.org/pdf/2010/lessons_indonesia_fossil_fuel_reform.pdf [31 Aug. 2016].

Bender, K.; Knoss, J. 2011. "Social protection reform in Indonesia. In search of universal coverage", in Practitioners' Perspectives, Part 4, pp. 327-338.

Hidayat, B.; Mundiharno; Němec, J.; Rabovskaja, V.; Rozanna, C.S.; Spatz, J. 2015. Financial sustainability of Indonesian health insurance (Jakarta, Indonesian-German Social Protection Programme (SPP)).

Huck-ju, K.; Woo-rim, K. 2015. "The evolution of cash transfers in Indonesia: Policy transfer and national adaptation", in Asia & the Pacific Policy Studies, Vol. 2, No. 2, pp. 425-440.

Sumarto, S.; Bazzi, S. 2011. Social protection in Indonesia: Past experiences and lessons for the future, Paper presented at the 2011 Annual Bank Conference on Development Opportunities (ABCDE) jointly organized by the World Bank and OECD, 30 May-1 June 2011, Paris.

World Bank. 2012. Indonesia social assistance program and public expenditure review (Jakarta).

13

Myanmar: National dialogue process[21]

The Assessment-based National Dialogue (ABND) process in Myanmar helped to develop a consensus on the picture of the existing social protection situation in the country. This included identification of social protection schemes administered by the central Government, challenges, policy recommendations and their estimated costs. The process encompassed several national dialogue workshops which debated and decided on concrete policy recommendations to establish a social protection floor (SPF) in Myanmar.

The ABND process conducted during 2013-15 convened a wide range of social protection stakeholders, such as:
- Ministries of Social Welfare, Relief and Resettlement; Labour, Employment and Social Security; Health; Finance; Education; Livestock, Fisheries and Rural Development; National Planning and Economic Development; and Home Affairs;
- workers' and employers' representatives;
- development agencies, such as ILO, IOM, UNAIDS, UNFPA, UNDP, UNICEF, UNOPS, WHO, WFP, JICA, World Bank;
- non-governmental organizations (NGOs); and
- research institutions.

---

[21] This chapter was authored by Lou Tessier of the ILO and reviewed by Valérie Schmitt and Loveleen De of the ILO. It was first published in September 2016.

1. Main lessons learned

- The ABND process helped to define the SPF in Myanmar and provide inputs to the National Social Protection Strategic Plan, policy discussions on the Rural Development Strategic Framework and universal health coverage.
- At the time of conducting the ABND, Myanmar was in a post-conflict setting and undergoing a transition to full democracy. Against this backdrop, the ABND successfully facilitated participatory dialogue on social policy among ministries and development partners.
- The cost of providing an SPF to all people in the country was estimated, which can form a basis for prioritizing the policy recommendations and exploring the mobilization of fiscal resources.
- The ABND was harmonized with other social protection activities undertaken in Myanmar, such as the World Bank's social protection inventory. This encouraged collaboration between development partners under the auspices of the Social Protection Inter-Agency Cooperation Board (SPIAC-B), based on mutual synergies.

2. What was the ABND process and its outcomes?

Step 1 – Building the assessment matrix: The ABND assessment matrix was prepared based on an inventory of social protection schemes developed by the World Bank. The matrix describes the social protection schemes in Myanmar that are administered by the central Government and compares them with the SPF guarantees to identify gaps and challenges.

The matrix was reviewed at the first national dialogue workshop held 23-25 March 2014. The outcome of the workshop was a consensus on the social protection provisions in Myanmar, gaps in coverage, implementation issues and policy recommendations to address these issues and establish an SPF for all people throughout their life cycles.

Step 2 – Costing the SPF: A second national dialogue workshop was held during 18-20 June 2014 to translate the recommendations into practical policy options in order to estimate their costs. The costing exercise was facilitated by the ILO and received inputs from the UN country team, ministries and NGOs.

Figure 18: Cost of SPF in Myanmar as % of GDP, 2018-24

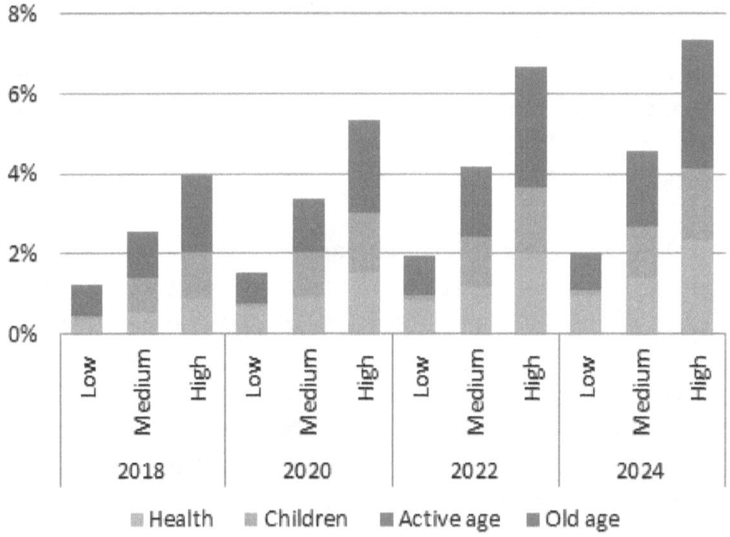

Source: ILO, 2015.

A third national dialogue workshop was held during 3-5 September 2014. The workshop included training on using a costing model called the Rapid Assessment Protocol (RAP) and a review of the policy options. The outcome was the estimated cost of three SPF packages (low, medium and high) depending on national priorities. The SPF package of benefits was estimated to cost between 2.2 and 7.2 per cent of gross domestic product (GDP) once it has been fully implemented by 2024, as shown in Figure 18.

Following the costing of the SPF, simulations were done to estimate the impact of the SPF on poverty reduction in the country. The simulations suggest that the SPF has the potential to reduce poverty incidence by 13 per cent and a universal social health protection scheme can reduce poverty incidence by 4.3 per cent.

Financing the SPF would involve mobilizing additional fiscal resources. At present, government revenues in Myanmar rely heavily on revenues of state-owned enterprises and proceeds from the sale of licences to international companies entering the local market. Fiscal resource mobilization could be done through several means, such as budgetary reallocations, changes in the government revenue structure, introduction of taxes, among other means. This is important to ensure the sustainable financing of the SPF.

Step 3 – Launching the ABND report: The ABND report was produced in September 2014 and provided inputs to the drafting of the National Social Protection Strategic Plan. This Plan includes eight new flagship programmes for the extension of social protection, which are all policy options developed through the ABND process. It was adopted in December 2014 under the leadership of the Ministry of Social Welfare, Relief and Resettlement. The final ABND report was launched in May 2015 and was further used in several policy discussions, such as those on the Rural Development Strategic Framework, universal health coverage and an Essential Package of Health Services for all.

3. How did the ABND exercise capitalize on mutual synergies?

In Myanmar, the national dialogue process capitalized on the mutual synergies and resources of different development agencies. This was done by coordinating the different social protection tools being used by agencies. For instance, the ILO, World Food Programme and the World Bank worked together to combine the United Nations' ABND methodology and the SPIAC-B's Social Protection Assessment (SPA) tools. The SPA inventory of existing social protection provisions informed the first step of the ABND, which included listing existing social protection schemes, issues and policy recommendations. Likewise, the national dialogue process, which forms the core component of the ABND, offered a platform to discuss the results of the SPA tool.

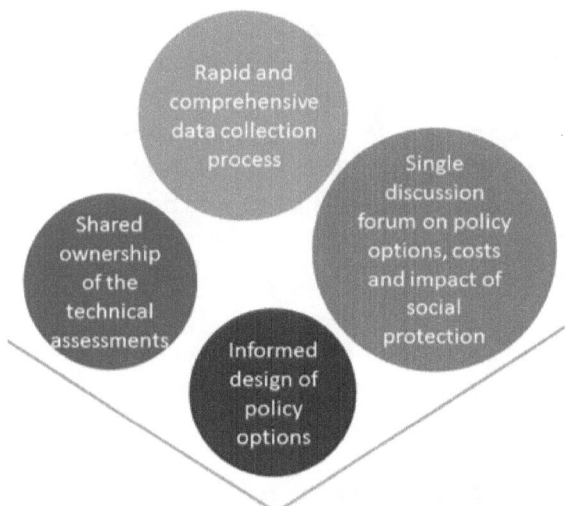

High-impact technical products and platform for sectoral coordination

This had some positive effects. It helped to capitalize on mutual strengths and avoid duplication of effort. Cooperation between agencies allowed them to share the workload of data collection and avoid fatigue among key stakeholders. It also fostered shared ownership of the different tools. The development partners were able to provide relevant and impactful technical inputs to the policy-making process in Myanmar through a participatory process with the ultimate objective to move towards making basic social protection a reality for all people in the country.

The information collected for the ABND matrix was made available online to avoid discrepancies in the data and figures used by various stakeholders.[22] As a result, the stakeholders agreed on a baseline for monitoring progress as the extension of social protection moves forward.

Application of the different social protection tools also facilitated the development of the National Social Protection Strategic Plan, which includes eight flagship social protection schemes proposed by the ABND process. To make the Plan a reality and implement an SPF in the country, further work is required to assess its fiscal implications. Greater and improved coordination among ministries is also needed. For this to be done, the results of the ABND and SPA tools can be used as a basis for further discussions, analysis and decision-making.

4. What's next?

Extending the coverage of social protection schemes to all people in Myanmar could be done through three steps, as described below.

Mobilizing sustainable fiscal space: The recommendations from the ABND process can be used to advocate to the Government to make impactful investments in the social protection system. Building the national social protection system through fiscal investments can help to ensure sustainability of the system. A detailed expenditure review can be conducted to identify ways to generate fiscal resources for social protection. Furthermore, prioritization of the recommendations and a phased implementation plan can help to ease the burden on fiscal resources.

Scaling up existing schemes and implementing new schemes: Detailed feasibility studies and legal reviews need to be done in order to implement or extend national social protection

---

[22] www.social-protection.org/gimi/gess/ShowProject.action?id=3010

schemes and ensure their sustainability. The implementation can be done in an efficient, cost-effective and transparent way through the use of technology.

Strengthening sectoral coordination to aid benefit delivery: Coordination among different institutions needs to be improved, which could be facilitated by the multi-stakeholder working platform established by the ABND process. This can help to synchronize the identification of beneficiaries and the delivery of benefits to avoid fragmentation and duplication of efforts. The platform can also be used to design the architecture of an integrated delivery system to improve access to social protection.

5. References

Government of Myanmar. 2014. Myanmar National Social Protection Strategic Plan.

—. 2014. Myanmar Rural Development Strategic Framework.

—. 2014. Myanmar Health Vision 2030.

ILO; WFP; Wold Bank. 2015. ILO-WFP-World Bank collaboration in Myanmar to support the expansion of social protection, joint ILO-WFP-World Factsheet.

Tessier, L. 2015. Towards a social protection floor in Myanmar: Assessment-based National Dialogue (Myanmar, ILO and UNCT). Available at: www.social-protection.org/gimi/gess/ShowRessource.action?ressource.ress ourceId=52460.

UNICEF. 2013. Towards child-focused social investments, Snapshot of Social Sector Public Budget Allocations and Spending in Myanmar (Myanmar).

World Bank. Myanmar Social Protection Note Series. Available at: http://documents.worldbank.org/curated/en/home.

14

Mongolia: Financing social protection through taxation of natural resources[23]

Mongolia is an example of a country that has recently started to take more advantage of its vast natural resources. Mongolia's development has been spurred by revenues from extractive industries. The Government has made significant efforts to ensure that the wealth created from its natural resources is shared among the wider population and that resources are directed to social protection programmes, such as the Universal Child Money programme.

Natural resources in resource-rich countries can create a basis for development and support social and socio-economic spending, technological advancement, foreign direct investment and overall economic growth.

Experiences from developing countries, such as Bolivia, Brazil, Chile, Argentina, Colombia, Botswana, Zambia, Indonesia and Malaysia, as well as those of developed countries, including Australia, Canada, Norway, Sweden and the United States, show that natural resource extraction can have positive impacts on socio-economic outcomes.

---

[23] This chapter was authored by Stefan Urban of the ILO and reviewed by Isabel Ortiz and Hiroshi Yamabana of the ILO. It was first published in August 2016.

1. Main lessons learned

- Natural resource-rich countries can boost their social protection system through the taxation of natural resources, thus increasing government revenues to support increased social protection expenditures.
- Directly linking government revenues generated from natural resources to funds allocated to social protection programmes helps to redistribute wealth created from natural resources to the wider population.
- Through the taxation of natural resources and the expansion of social protection spending, the Government managed to significantly reduce poverty rates.
- Efforts to increase transparency and operational efficiency at all levels of the Government further support the allocation of funds to social expenditures.
- The establishment of a stabilization fund would further help in balancing volatility in government revenues due to natural resource price fluctuations.

2. The risk of natural resource abundance

Even though some countries have fared well, the impact of natural resource abundance is not always clear and predictable. In some cases, abundant natural resources have been a curse rather than a blessing, resulting in large-scale corruption, strengthening of authoritarian rules and environmental damage. Exploitation of mineral resources in the Democratic Republic of the Congo and oil in Nigeria, Angola and Equatorial Guinea offers clear examples of misappropriation of extractive industry revenues. Lopsided growth due to the "Dutch disease" can further lead to the crowding out of other sectors and make the national economy less competitive due to currency appreciation, making exports more expensive and less competitive.

Successful cases offer lessons on what to avoid and emulate when a developing country's economy is based heavily on natural resource extraction. Common elements observed in countries that have successfully developed with the help of natural resource extractive industries include: introducing elements of revenue redistribution; linking natural resource rents and taxes to social and socio-economic investments and development; strengthening tax authorities; increasing transparency; and improving governance structures.

3. Taxing natural resource extraction in Mongolia

The Mongolian economy has experienced positive economic growth, with an average growth rate of around 8.4 per cent between 2005 and 2015, making it one of the fastest growing economies in the world. In parallel, the poverty rate has been on a downward trend from 38.8 per cent in 2010 to 21.6 per cent in 2014.

Mongolia, especially in relation to its population of 2.9 million, is rich in natural resources. The country's gold and copper reserves are among the largest in the world. The estimated value of total natural resource reserves that have been identified to date is US$1.3 trillion. Mongolia's natural resources include copper, gold, coal, molybdenum, iron ore, uranium, tin, tungsten, silver, zinc and fluorspar.

The Government of Mongolia applies royalty rates of 5 per cent on natural resource extraction. In addition, there is a 10 per cent corporate income tax on profits and surcharges in the form of progressive royalty rates and exploration and production licencing fees.

Over the past decade, natural resource extraction boomed. In 2010, the extractive sector accounted for 30 per cent of GDP, 32 per cent of government revenues and 81 per cent of exports, with an employment share of 5 per cent of the total workforce.

Government revenues have increased significantly since the expansion of natural resource extraction operations.

There have been visible efforts to increase transparency and operational efficiency at all levels of the Government. Mongolia joined the Extractive Industries Transparency Initiative, received a full compliance status in 2010 and has reported its revenues on a regular basis.

4. Natural resource extraction revenues and social protection

Several initiatives have been launched in Mongolia during the last decade, aimed at linking revenues collected from the natural resource extraction industry to social protection programmes, thereby redistributing wealth created from natural resources to the wider population.

A. Mongolian Development Fund (MDF)

In July 2006, the Government introduced universal child benefits. In parallel, windfall profits taxes were introduced to capture a higher share of mining profits. All revenues created from natural resource extraction (dividends and 70 per cent of royalties) entered the newly created Mongolian Development Fund (MDF). This was the Government's first attempt to create a sovereign wealth fund. The fund had several functions: stabilize unplanned budget deficits; undertake investments aimed at increasing domestic economic capacity; support small and medium-sized enterprises; and support children and families through the universal child benefit scheme.

The MDF was the Government's first effort to legislate the link between government resource receipts and cash transfers. In January 2007, the MDF significantly increased the annual benefit amount of the Universal Child Money programme from 36,000 Mongolian Tughriks (MNT) (US$30.76) to MNT136,000 to ($116.19) per child.

B. Human Development Fund (HDF)

In 2009, following the 2008 elections and after the initial turmoil caused by the financial crisis that significantly affected natural resource prices, the MDF was replaced by the Human Development Fund (HDF). The mandate of the Fund, similar to the previous one, was to create and grow sustainable resources for better income distribution among the population. The HDF had the same function as the MDF but on a much larger scale. The legislation did not limit benefits and included health insurance and pensions, housing payments, cash and medical and education service payments. A cash transfer amount was set at MNT120,000 ($89.08) per person in 2010. The total cost of the schemes was three times as much as the Universal Child Money programme in 2009. The new schemes under the HDF were generous and came under pressure after income did not meet expenditures. The fund was temporarily replaced by a targeted poverty benefit programme.

Currently, the Government is considering the establishment of a sovereign wealth fund called the Future Heritage Fund. The fund is proposed to be operational as of 2018 and will replace the HDF. The idea is highly controversial and critics are questioning its benefits as it diverts funds away from social investments. The fund is expected to invest resources in international capital markets rather than on people and national development.

Alternatively, a stabilization fund could help mitigate the risk of market and price volatility and help the Government maintain a higher degree of liquidity during economic downturns and mineral price drops. As a result the Government is more likely to be in a position to balance social investments in the long run.

The Economic and Social Stabilization Fund of Chile is a good example of how to maintain liquidity and balance public expenditures. The stabilization fund is a countercyclical tool that aims to smooth government expenditures, finance fiscal deficits in times of low growth and/or low copper prices and to pay down public debt when necessary. Funds can be withdrawn from the Economic and Social Stabilization Fund at any time in order to fill budget gaps in public expenditures and to pay down public debt.

A high degree of fiscal flexibility is maintained by investing in portfolios with a high level of liquidity and low credit risk and volatility. The fund is invested up to 30 per cent in money market instruments, 66.5 per cent in sovereign bonds and 3.5 per cent in inflation-indexed sovereign bonds. The Chilean Economic and Stabilisation fund represents a model for Latin America and could be applied in other countries that face similar market volatilities.

5. Conclusion

Mongolia presents a case where government revenues generated from the taxation of companies engaged in natural resource extraction have been directed to social protection programmes. The Government was successful in redistributing some of the wealth from extractive industries.

Taxing natural resource extraction is one of the many alternatives that countries have to expand fiscal space for social protection. Governments normally use a mix of taxes and social security contributions to fund social protection, combined with other options explained in the paper, "Fiscal space for social protection: Options to expand social investments in 187 countries".

6. References

Columbia Center on Sustainable Investment. 2013. Chile: The pension reserve fund and the economic and social stabilization fund. Available at:
http://ccsi.columbia.edu/files/2014/04/nrf_Chile_August2013_R WI_VCC.pdf [31 Aug. 2016].

Ernst, C. Forthcoming. Revenues from extractive industries: An opportunity to finance sustainable social spending (Geneva, International Labour Organization).

Extractive Industries Transparency Initiative. 2015. Mongolia ninth EITI reconciliation report 2014 (Ulaanbaatar, Working group of the Mongolia Extractive Industries Transparency Initiative).

Isakova, A.; Plekhanov, A.; Zettelmeyer, J. 2012. Managing Mongolia`s resource boom, Working Paper No. 138 (London, European Bank for Reconstruction and Development).

Ministry of Finance Mongolia. 2015. Extractive industry fiscal regime in Mongolia, Presented at the natural resource taxation conference in Jakarta. Available at: http://www.imf.org/external/np/seminars/eng/2015/natrestax/pdf/batbayar.pdf [31 Aug. 2016].

Chimeddorj, O. 2015. Managing revenues from extractive industry: The case of Mongolia. Available at: https://www.unpei.org/system/files_force/Mining%20Revenue-edited_final%20draft.pdf?download=1 [31 Aug. 2016].

Moran, T.H. 2013. Avoiding the "resource curse" in Mongolia, Policy Brief Number PB13-18 (Washington, DC, Peterson Institute for International Economics).

Ortiz, I.; Cummins, M.; Karunanethy, K. 2015. Fiscal space for social protection: Options to expand social investments in 187 countries, ESS Working Paper No. 48, (Geneva, International Labour Office).

Yeung, Y., Howes, S. 2015. Resources-to-cash: A cautionary tale from Mongolia, Action Research Report (Canberra, Development Policy Center, Australian National University).

15

Mongolia: One Stop Shop[24]

The One-Stop-Shop (OSS) is a response to the challenge of providing accessible, transparent, efficient and quality social services in Mongolia, the most sparsely populated country in the world.

Starting in 2007 and implemented nation-wide since 2013, the One-Stop-Shops (OSSs) deliver social protection and employment counseling services, as well as notary and banking services at aimag (provincial) and soum (district) levels.

Gathering representatives from different government agencies (including social insurance, social welfare, and employment departments), the OSS has offered the Government an opportunity to enhance the legal framework of public service provision and improve accessibility, awareness, and transparency of services provided.

Now commonly used by the population, the OSS provides an opportunity for local administrations to improve coordination and the quality of public services provided to their population.

1. Main lessons learned

- Even the most sparsely populated country in the world can guarantee universal access to social protection to its population.

---

[24] This chapter was authored by Thibault van Langenhove and Céline Peyron-Bista of the ILO and reviewed by Isabel Ortiz and Valérie Schmitt of the ILO. It was first published in August 2015.

- The OSS is a single delivery point that enables people to access information on existing programmes and avail social services and transfers. It therefore contributes to the extension of social protection coverage.
- In addition, mobile OSSs deliver services at the doorsteps of those who cannot travel to an OSS facility, such as older people or herders who cannot leave their livestock.
- With a common delivery point for all programmes, the OSS enhances coordination between institutions in charge of social protection and employment promotion while reducing duplication and inefficiencies. It also diminishes the dichotomy between social welfare and social insurance and fosters the creation of a comprehensive social protection system.
- The OSS could be used to establish a common monitoring and evaluation system of the social protection system and local development plans.

2. **The challenge of delivering quality services in remote areas of the most sparsely populated country in the world**

With a population of 2.8 million inhabitants and a density of less than two people per square kilometre, Mongolia is the most sparsely populated country in the world. Driven mainly by the mining sector, Mongolia's economy has grown rapidly in recent years.

Mongolia has a well-developed social protection system (social insurance, social welfare, and active labour market policies), providing social benefits and employment services to people at each stage of life. In 2012, 97.8 per cent of the population was covered by the Social Health Insurance Fund (mandatory insurance subsidized for specific and vulnerable groups).

However, delivering social services and transfers across a very sparsely populated country is challenging. In many cases obtaining a public administrative service in Mongolia requires visiting several service-providing departments, which can be located at considerable distances from each other. Therefore, applying for services can be time-consuming, entail transportation costs and, in the case of citizens traveling from remote soums (rural districts) to aimag (provincial) centres, additional costs, such as boarding and lodging. Moreover, information is sometimes inaccurate, insufficient, and/or difficult to obtain.

Launched in 2007 with support from the Swiss Development Cooperation and implemented by the Human Security Policy Study Centre, a non-governmental organization (NGO), the One-Stop-Shop (OSS) Project established facilities where citizens can receive several kinds of public services and a number of privately delivered notary and banking services. These accessible and customer-oriented "one-stop shops" aimed to increase accessibility, transparency, and efficiency of public service delivery, as well as reduce corruption and transaction costs.

Based on this initial pilot project, the OSS was extended to the whole country in 2013 by adoption of Government Decree No. 153 and its related Regulation on One-Stop-Shop activities.

3. Officers from different schemes and programmes gather in a single room at the local government office

The main feature of the OSS in Mongolia is that it brings together, in one unique room, officers from different social protection schemes, employment programmes, and other public and private services. As stated by Decree No. 153 of 2013 on the establishment of OSSs, such facilities are to be implemented in all administrative sub-divisions of Mongolia: Ulaanbaatar districts, khoroos (sub-divisions of Ulaanbaatar districts), aimags (provinces), and soums (rural districts). In each location, the OSS is placed under the responsibility of the Head of the Governor's Office.

All following schemes, programmes, and services need to be represented in the OSS facility:

- social insurance;
- social welfare;
- employment promotion;
- land management;
- civil registration; and
- bank and notary services.

To answer specific local needs, additional services can also be included in the OSS (e.g. veterinary and livestock services).

Officers working in the OSS are civil servants and salaried workers of the schemes, programmes, and services they represent. They report directly to their institutions of origin and there is no reporting line between them and the Head of the Governor's Office. The latter is responsible for ensuring the smooth functioning of the OSS facility.

To increase access to services and deliver services at the doorsteps of those beneficiaries who cannot travel (e.g. older persons, herders), a mobile OSS facility (a van) was piloted in 2011 in Bagakhangai district of Ulaanbaatar.

Mobile OSSs are now being extended to two additional aimags, with the objective to scale-up the initiative and provide government services to all the most remote areas of the country.

4. Thanks to the OSS, public services are more accessible

Over 60 per cent of Mongolia's population uses the OSS on a regular basis. In 2011, 31 established OSSs served more than 1.8 million customers, including over 600,000 customers in

Ulaanbaatar City and over 1.2 million customers in rural areas. Based on an internal survey conducted in 2011, the satisfaction rate with OSS services was 85 per cent.

The concentration of many administrative services in one location has enabled customers to save time and money in accessing services. Regarding the social protection sector, the implementation of the OSS has resulted in the clarification and simplification of application and claim processes. The description of the different steps to avail benefits is detailed in guides for citizens that are available at the OSS. Additionally, many local administrations have installed a telephone hotline that allows citizens to access accurate information about services and the necessary documents needed when visiting the OSS.

The proximity between the different officers within the OSS facility has also led to better coordination between the social welfare agency, the social insurance scheme, and employment promotion services. In some localities, memorandums of understanding (MOUs) have been signed between these different organizations in order to offer combined benefit packages that better address the needs of households and reduce poverty more effectively.

5. Next Steps

The implementation of OSSs is not yet complete in each khoroo (sub-district of Ulanbaatar) and soum (rural district). Hence, there is room for the Government to further enforce Regulation No. 153 of 2013, building on the successes already achieved and accumulated experience.

Vertical coordination between OSSs that exist at different administrative layers and horizontal coordination with pre-existing line divisions from centralized schemes would also benefit from being further clarified. At present, OSSs and local divisions of schemes are competing to attract recipients. A list of services available in the OSSs at different layers within the administration could be introduced in order to ensure consistency across the OSSs and their complementarity with services provided by other existing divisions.

Today each OSS officer manages its own registry of beneficiaries without sharing it with other officers from other schemes and programmes. The development of a single beneficiary database with a unique identification system would further simplify administrative processes, enhance possible synergies between programmes, and give way to a common monitoring and evaluation system that could be used for national reporting and the improvement of local development plans.

Finally, despite important efforts and encouraging results, processes for enrolling in programmes and claiming benefits remain quite complex compared to other countries. There might be a need to further simplify the administrative procedures from a user's point of view, thus promoting more cooperation between the different components of the administration.

6. References

ILO. 2015. Mongolia: Assessment based national dialogue on social protection and employment promotion. Workspace on the ILO social protection platform. Available at: www.social-protection.org/gimi/gess/ShowProject.action?id=2287.

Peyron-Bista, C; Amgalan, L.; Sanjjav, B.; Tumurtulga, B. 2015. Assessment based national dialogue on social protection: Definition and cost of a social protection floor in Mongolia (Ulaanbaatar, ILO).

van Langenhove, T. 2015. Fact-findings, local assessment report and recommendations for the further development of the OSS, 2015 (ILO working document).

Swiss Agency for Development and Cooperation. 2013. Factsheet – Governance and decentralisation programme: Module 4.1. (Ulaanbaatar). Available at:
www.eda.admin.ch/content/dam/countries/countries-content/mongolia/en/resource_en_229882.pdf.

—. 2013. Swiss Cooperation Strategy, Mongolia, 2013-2016. (Bern). Available at:
www.eda.admin.ch/content/dam/countries/countries-content/mongolia/en/resource_en_219861.pdf.

—. 2015. Project webpage. Available at:
www.eda.admin.ch/countries/mongolia/en/home/international-cooperation/projects.html/content/projects/SDC/en/2012/7F08 183/phase2.html?oldPagePath=/content/countries/mongolia/en/home/internationale-zusammenarbeit/projekte.html.

16

South Africa: Integrated Community Registration Outreach Programme[25]

The Integrated Community Registration Outreach Programme (ICROP) for socially excluded people in rural and semi-urban areas of South Africa has considerably improved people's effective access to existing social services and benefits.

Despite the existence of basic social services and benefits in South Africa, a significant number of people did not have effective access. This situation led the South African Social Security Agency (SASSA) to consider a more integrated and intensive approach to reach excluded people. As a result, mobile units were dispatched to deliver the Child Support Grant (CSG) in 2001. This programme was the predecessor of ICROP, which was launched in 2007.

ICROP is an outreach programme delivering social services through fully equipped mobile one-stop service units, or vehicles equipped with modern technology, facilities, and personnel. Its objective is to promote development, poverty reduction, and social inclusion for isolated people.

---

[25] This chapter was authored by Frank Earl and Pathamavathy Naicker of the South Africa Social Security Agency, and Clara van Panhuys and Tomás Barbero of the ILO and reviewed by Isabel Ortiz, Valérie Schmitt, Christina Behrendt and Loveleen De of the ILO. It was first published in September 2016.

1. Main lessons learned

- A concrete set of measures, such as those that make up ICROP, ensure the accessibility and adequacy of existing benefits and services and effectively extend social protection coverage.
- The use of mobile units and the latest available technology has proven to be effective in reaching out to excluded communities in rural and geographically isolated areas.
- Delivery of social protection programmes and services across the country follows a standardized approach both in areas targeted by ICROP and areas where fixed service points and local offices facilitate delivery. As a result, service delivery became more effective and efficient while administrative costs were reduced. However, these results required good coordination across institutions, processes, and tools at the national and decentralized levels.

2. How was ICROP set up?

The South African Constitution stipulates that "everyone has a right to have access to social security, including, if they are unable to support themselves and their dependants, appropriate social assistance".

Since 1996, government priorities included eliminating poverty and reducing inequality, unemployment, mass deprivation, and serious service delivery lags. Redistribution of resources through cash transfers became the country's main poverty reduction strategy. South Africa also provides free primary health care for all, school nutrition, and fee waivers for poor students.

Despite the existence of social protection programmes, between 2001 and 2007 there were no major improvements in poverty and deprivation indexes (where deprivation was measured along five dimensions, including income and material, employment, education, biological parents, and service delivery), particularly in rural and semi-rural areas (Barnes et al., 2007). An evaluation of social interventions showed the need to expand and improve the delivery of social services and transfers.

Concerned with these findings, SASSA decided to launch ICROP in 2007 in order to institutionalize and expand the existing successful CSG outreach programme. Since the President's launch of the 'war on poverty' in 2008, ICROP has evolved into a government-wide programme that takes all services in an integrated manner to the most excluded people.

3. What does ICROP look like?

ICROP aims to reach out to socially excluded and isolated people and communities in order to ensure accessibility, availability, adequacy, affordability, and acceptability of social services and benefits. ICROP primarily targets deep rural, rural and semi-urban areas, which were the most socially excluded and isolated areas in terms of the 2007 deprivation index.

Through fully equipped and well-staffed mobile units and other outreach services, ICROP:

- facilitates beneficiary enrolment and registration processes, and issues smart cards that give access to benefits;
- identifies beneficiaries through biometric (fingerprint and voice) recognition since 2013;
- updates a web-based beneficiary database in real-time or within 7-21 working days, depending on connectivity;
- raises awareness and provides information on existing benefits and services;
- provides access to pay points where smart cards can be used at a minimal cost and with reduced waiting periods. ICROP does not pay the grants. The grant payment system is outsourced to a private company and the benefit amounts can be retrieved at accredited merchants, ATMs, banks, or pay points;

- facilitates access to the appeals process, including applications for representation to appeal against the decision to terminate benefits; and
- conducts home visits by medical staff and social workers to ensure that individuals unable to go to the hospital or leave their homes, due to disability or sickness, have access to services and benefits.

Figure 19: Programmes covered by ICROP in South Africa

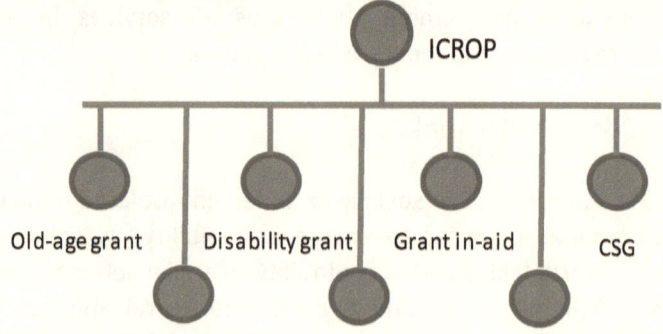

Source: SASSA website.

The lead agency for social protection programme implementation is SASSA, which falls under the Department of Social Development. Other departments, including Home Affairs, Health, Justice, Education, Agriculture, and Cooperative Governance, as well as local municipalities, are involved in programme delivery. The police are involved to ensure safety and security. An inter-ministerial committee facilitates coordination across departments. Although decisions are made at the central level, delivery occurs at the provincial, district, and local levels through local offices, pay points, or ICROP mobile units. The benefits provided by SASSA are rights-based and implemented according to uniform standards governed by a solid legal framework.

The budget for ICROP is allocated by Parliament and managed according to the Public Finance Management Act. The programme is funded from tax revenues. For 2013-14, the budget was approximately 4.5 billion rands (ZAR) (US$481 million). ICROP expenditures mainly include vehicle maintenance costs and staff costs.

4. The impact of ICROP on people's lives

In 2011, about 45 per cent of the country's total population was concentrated in rural areas, of which 20 per cent lived in deep rural areas. A recent study indicates that in rural areas targeted by the ICROP programme, the proportion of the population effectively covered by existing social protection programmes was high compared to the estimated target population (UNICEF, 2011). Between 2007 and 2013, ICROP served over 730 wards and completed more than 320,000 applications for children to access the Child Support Grant.

Figure 20: Cumulative Child Grant registrations through ICROP in South Africa

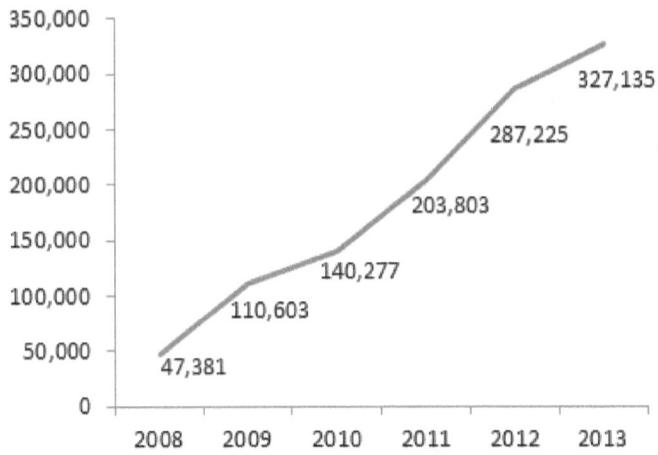

Source: UNICEF, 2013.

The ultimate aim of ICROP is to contribute to poverty reduction. It is interesting to note that as a result of increasing beneficiary inclusion rates for existing social protection programmes since the introduction of ICROP in 2007, the poverty headcount ratio decreased from 57.2 per cent in 2006 to 45.5 per cent in 2011 (World Bank).

ICROP also aims to make beneficiaries financially independent by providing opportunities for skills development, employment, and entrepreneurship through small public employment initiatives. For example, SASSA's Social Relief of Distress programme awards food purchased from local garden producers and school uniforms purchased from local cooperatives to destitute individuals within the community. Hence, the initiative not only benefits children and families, but also enhances local economic growth and sustainable development within poor communities.

5. What's next?

ICROP has significantly improved the access of rural populations and persons with disabilities to existing grants. However, a few challenges yet remain:

- The programme was designed without considering physical impediments. For example, in some cases the vehicles are too large to reach communities. It is important to assess how to best reach out to these communities.
- SASSA needs to further invest in training for the staff of the mobile ICROP units who are in direct contact with the beneficiaries.
- ICROP initiatives aimed at increasing beneficiaries' economic independence initially faced difficulties since they would have involved assessing and providing financial opportunities to more than 8 million people. The approach recently changed and now focuses on smaller scale projects. Projects promoting linkages between social grants and employment or skills development initiatives should be encouraged and enhanced.
- SASSA needs to adapt its strategies to enhance its service delivery to poor people in affluent provinces and

urban areas where the number of potential beneficiaries that do not have effective access to existing social grants has increased in recent years. Services may be available in these areas, but are insufficient and understaffed.

- An institutionalized mechanism for service delivery audits, public consultations, and collection of feedback needs to be designed and established to assess satisfaction and improve the delivery system.
- Several reforms are being initiated as part of the extension of a national social protection floor, which may lead to the establishment of new schemes. ICROP needs to be ready to support the effective delivery of these potential new services and transfers.

6. References

Aguero, J.M.; Carter, M.R.; Woolard, I. 2007. The impact of unconditional cash transfers on nutrition: The South Africa Child Support Grant, International Working Paper No. 39 (Brasilia, International Poverty Centre). Available at: http://www.ipc-undp.org/pub/IPCWorkingPaper39.pdf.

Barnes, H.; Wright, G.; Noble, M.; Dawes, A. 2007. South African index of multiple deprivation for children, census 2001 (Cape Town, Human Sciences Research Council Press). Available at: http://www.casasp.ox.ac.uk/docs/The%20South%20African%20Index%20of%20Multiple%20Deprivation%20for%20Children.pdf.

Committee of Inquiry. 2002. Transforming the present, protecting the future (Pretoria, Department of Social Development). Available at:
www.cdhaarmann.com/Publications/Taylor%20report.pdf.

Customer Care Department. 2007. ICROP Strategy (Pretoria, SASSA).

Department of Social Development website. Available at: www.dsd.gov.za.

National Planning Commission. 2013. National Development Plan, 2030 (Pretoria, national Planning Commission).

National Treasury Republic of South Africa. 2013. Medium Term Budget Policy Statement 2013 (Pretoria, National Treasury). Available at: www.treasury.gpg.gov.za/

Operations Department. 2012. Standardisation of Business Processes (Pretoria, SASSA).

The Presidency. 2008. War on poverty: Framework for implementation (Pretoria, the Presidency).

Samson, M. et al. 2004. Final report. The social and economic impact of South Africa's social security system (Cape Town, Economic Policy Research Institute). Available at: http://allafrica.com/download/resource/main/main/idatcs/0001 0352:3ca37b223f2ad1b0dc6479ccca726034.pdf

SASSA website. Available at: www.sassa.gov.za.

SASSA and UNICEF. 2013. Preventing exclusion from the Child Support Grant: A study of exclusion errors in accessing CSG benefits (Pretoria: UNICEF South Africa). Available at: www.unicef.org/southafrica/resources_14005.html

World Bank Global Poverty Working Group, online database. Available at: http://data.worldbank.org/country/south-africa. Accessed on 2 March 2015.

17

South Africa: Anchoring rights in law[26]

The South African social protection system is one of the most comprehensive within the region. Its statutory and effective coverage rates are above the region's average and comparable or even beyond those of other BRICS countries. The comprehensive nature of the system lies in contributory and non-contributory cash and in-kind legal guarantees which form the country's national social protection floor; these can be attributed to national political commitment to curb poverty, effective institutions and delivery systems, sound fiscal basis and adequate funding. The system relies on three pillars: social assistance; mandatory social insurance; and voluntary private insurance. The Constitution, characterized by its broad-ranging social and economic rights including the entrenched right to social security, has played a key role in the development of the social security system.

1. Main lessons learned

- South Africa's experience shows that the Constitution, when it is given effect through the implementation of a strong legal framework, can play a pivotal role in establishing a comprehensive social protection system.
- South Africa's experience also shows that legal and effective coverage can be achieved through a mix of

---

[26] This chapter was authored by Maya Stern-Plaza and Geneviève Binette of the ILO and reviewed by Isabel Ortiz, Valérie Schmitt, Luis Frota and Kagisanyo Kelobang of the ILO. It was first published in September 2016.

        social assistance and contributory social protection schemes that are anchored in a solid legal framework in line with international social security standards and a significant extension of social protection.

- The mix of schemes, in particular the introduction of rights-based social assistance programmes, has contributed to the effective and sustainable reduction of poverty and income inequality.
- South Africa's experience shows that International social security standards can provide a useful framework for the development and reform of national social security systems.

2. The right to social protection in the South African Constitution

South Africa has embraced a rights-based approach to social security. This flows from the provisions of the Constitution to the laws and implementing regulations that make up the social security legal framework.

The South African Bill of Rights (Chapter 2 of the Constitution, No. 108 of 1996) guarantees everyone's right to "have access to health care services, including reproductive health care; sufficient food and water", as well as the right to social security, including appropriate social assistance (article 27). In addition, "no one may be refused emergency medical treatment". The Constitution further requires the State to take reasonable measures, including legislative, within available resources, to achieve the progressive realization of each of these rights.

The constitutional right to social protection is given effect through the implementation of a legal framework that guarantees coverage of the population against the risks faced throughout the life cycle, both through social assistance programmes and contributory schemes. This legal framework also guarantees people's protection against poverty, vulnerability and social exclusion.

3. **Legal architecture of the South African social protection system**

A. **Access to health care**

Access to health care is granted either through the public health system funded through the budget (general taxes), or through contributory medical schemes, which cover employees in the public and private sectors. The National Health Insurance Act No. 61 of 2003 makes explicit reference to the right to health enshrined in the Bill of Rights. It establishes the national health system and the provision of health services, "including reproductive health care and emergency medical treatment, basic nutrition and basic health care services for children".

The public health system provides free primary health care (emergency, reproductive, immunization, family planning, tuberculosis treatment and sexually transmitted diseases, among others) to all residents whether national or non-national, including refugees and asylum seekers, thanks to jurisprudence emanating from the Constitutional Court. Other medical services require cost-sharing for households above an earnings threshold as set by the Ministry of Health in the approved Uniform Patient Fee Schedule. Those earning less than the threshold are either fully or partially subsidized or receive free medical care services. In addition, pregnant mothers, the disabled, pensioners and the indigent have access to free health services. The public health system is, however, under-resourced (both in terms of financial and human resources), particularly relative to the size of the population that it serves.

Contributory medical schemes provide access to private health-care facilities to 7 million people or 14 per cent of the population. Membership in these medical schemes and hospital care plans is not statutorily mandated, although it is frequently a condition of employment. The Medical Schemes Act 131 of 1998 provides a minimum package of benefits and regulates such contributory medical schemes.

The country spends far more than other middle-income countries on health care (8.5 per cent of gross domestic product (GDP) in 2014). However, health outcomes have been comparatively low primarily because of inequities between the public and private sectors. Discussion are currently ongoing over the possibility of introducing a comprehensive national health insurance (NHI) to provide all South Africans, irrespective of their employment status, equitable access to affordable and quality health care.

B.   Social protection for children and families

Income security for families with children is mainly provided by several tax-financed programmes.

The Social Assistance Act 13 of 2004 provides, among others, Child Support Grants, Care Dependency Grants and Foster Care Grants. South African citizens, permanent residents (i.e. a person who is lawfully and permanently resident in South Africa) and refugees (i.e. a person referred to in Section 1 of the Refugee Act, 1998) are covered by this scheme. The Child Support Grant is a means-tested non-contributory cash transfer targeted at children 0 to 18 years of age. The grant is provided to the primary caregiver of a child for up to a maximum of six children. It currently reaches more than 11 million children (out of a population of 19 million children) and is recognized as one of South Africa's most effective poverty reduction programmes.

The Care Dependency Grant provides for severely disabled children under the age of 18 who are in need of special care. The Foster Care Grant is the only non-means-tested grant. The purpose of the grant is to encourage families to foster children who would otherwise be placed in institutional care.

C. Social protection for women and men of working age

Income security for the working age is guaranteed through non-contributory and contributory schemes. The non-contributory scheme provides disability grants for women and men of working age. Persons of working age may access unemployment, sickness and maternity through the social insurance scheme or, in the case of employment injury, through a workers' compensation fund.

According to the Social Assistance Act 13 of 2004, disability grants are provided to beneficiaries aged 18-59 years who have sustained a non-occupational accident or disease resulting in permanent invalidity. The benefit is considered permanent if a citizen or permanent resident is assessed as medically disabled for more than 12 months. The benefit ceiling is currently set at 1,500 South African rands (ZAR) per month (approximately US$112).

Most benefits for women and men of working age are provided under the contributory system, the mandatory social insurance scheme in particular. Employees, including domestic workers, seasonal workers, mineworkers, formally employed agricultural workers and high-income earners, are entitled to unemployment, sickness and maternity benefits according to the Unemployment Insurance Act (UIA) of 2001 and the Unemployment Insurance Contributions Act 4 of 2002. Most atypical workers (i.e. independent contractors, dependent contractors and the self-employed), informal economy workers, the long-term unemployed, migrant workers and civil servants are excluded. The Unemployment Insurance Fund has proposed legislative changes to include some categories of excluded groups, including public servants, legal migrants and those in learnerships. Other changes would include increasing the benefit levels and duration.

Employment injury benefits are provided by the Workers Compensation Fund established by the Compensation for

Occupational Injuries and Diseases Act of 1993 (COIDA). The current legislation is more extensive and covers all employees (not only "workmen") for temporary disability benefits, permanent disability benefits, death benefits and medical expenses. Domestic workers, the unemployed and those in non-standard forms of work, such as the informally employed, self-employed and so-called dependent contractors, are excluded. Workers in the mining industry and related works receive lump sums under the Occupational Diseases in Mines and Works Act 78 of 1973 (ODMWA). There have been calls to merge both schemes to resolve a number of inconsistencies.

It may be noted that as a rule the South African social security system does not provide for the payment of death and survivors' benefits as a separate contingency. These are provided under a patchwork of legal provisions. Some may access survivors' benefits under COIDA or ODMWA where the loss of support suffered is the result of the death following an employment accident or disease. Otherwise survivors' spouses or life partners can access benefits under the UIA. Finally, the Pensions Funds Act 24 of 1956 provides survivors' benefits via retirement funds in the absence of a national pension scheme.

D.   Social protection for older women and men

South Africa does not have a national or public retirement fund scheme. Older persons have two main sources of income: the State's Older Person's Grant (OPG) and private pensions. Roughly two-thirds of South Africans do not contribute to a private pension, meaning they will rely on the OPG, their own private savings or support from relatives.

The Social Assistance Act 13 of 2004 sets out the entitlement conditions for access to the OPG, which is a means-tested grant provided to eligible pensioners aged 60 and over. Currently, nearly 3.2 million older persons receive this benefit (SASSA, 2016). In April 2016, the old-age grant was equal to ZAR1,500 (US$112) for pensioners aged 60-74 and ZAR1,520 (US$114) for pensioners aged 75 or older. Along with other grants, the OPG is one of the most important tools for poverty reduction in the country. This is evidenced by the reduction in the poverty incidence among older persons from 55.6 per cent in 2006 to 36.2 per cent in 2011.

Membership in private pension funds is not statutorily mandated; however, it is frequently a condition of employment. Private pension funds are primarily regulated by the Pension Funds Act 24 of 1956. The system is fragmented with close to 14,000 retirement funds. The Government has been considering pension reform. Reforms would include replacing the OPG with a universal basic pension that is accessible to all citizens and qualifying residents and including a mandatory contributory arrangement for the formal sector with legally guaranteed minimum benefits.

4. **Towards a comprehensive social protection legal framework based on international social security standards**

South Africa has established a comprehensive social protection system in line with a rights-based approach. The system is comprised of an extensive social assistance programme and a number of social insurance programmes underpinned by an entrenched Constitutional right to social security. This right is accompanied by the obligation to take reasonable legislative measures to achieve the progressive realization of the right to social security in line with international standards. This has resulted in a strong legal framework that encompasses several laws covering all contingencies foreseen in the Social Security (Minimum Standards) Convention, 1952 (No. 102). The Constitutional Court has also played a role in developing a substantial body of jurisprudence on the obligations imposed by the provisions of the Constitution, including the need to extend coverage to certain vulnerable groups.

In the field of social security, South Africa is a Party to the Unemployment Convention, 1919 (No. 2), as well as to the Equality of Treatment (Accident Compensation) Convention, 1925 (No. 19). In 2013, South Africa ratified the Domestic Workers Convention, 2011 (No. 189), which requires the State to ensure that domestic workers enjoy social security protection that is not less favourable than those applicable to workers generally. South Africa has not yet ratified the Social Security (Minimum Standards) Convention, 1952 (No. 102), although it has considered the possibility to do so.

Figure 21: South Africa's social protection legal framework

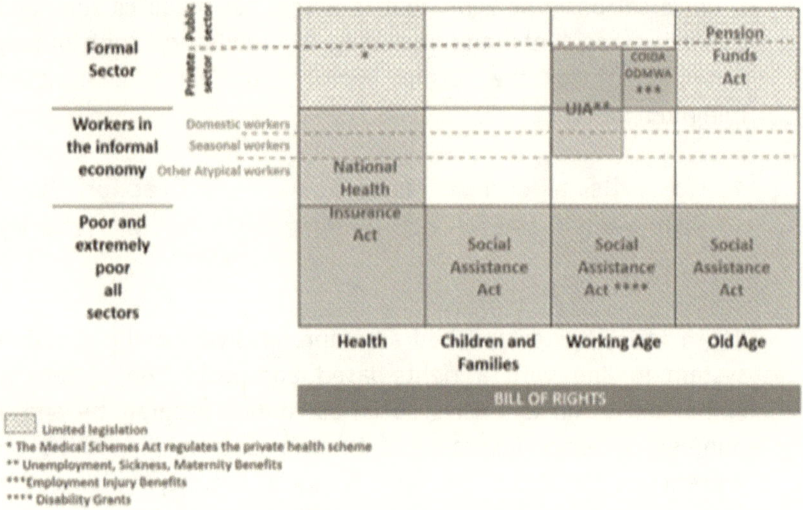

According to a comparative assessment undertaken by the ILO in 2014, South Africa would be in a position to ratify this landmark international standard and would be the first country to do so on the basis of its well-developed social assistance system. By ratifying Convention No. 102, South Africa would also establish itself as a model and an example for other southern African and African countries at large. Ratification would demonstrate South Africa's ongoing political will to effectively implement a coherent social security system as part of national development policies that are in line with the most recent international social security standard, the Social Protection Floors Recommendation, 2012 (No. 202).

While the South African social security scheme illustrates a good example of a comprehensive system, some challenges still need to be addressed. These include: overcoming administrative deficiencies in the granting of social assistance; addressing the country's high unemployment rate; and extending coverage to atypical workers, including workers in the informal economy, as well as the long-term unemployed and structurally unemployed youths and adults. Despite the fact that South Africa draws a good number of migrant workers from across the continent, temporary migrants do not have access to social assistance or UIA benefits. As such, extension should seek to fulfil the principles of "universality of protection and social inclusion" set in international standards. It can be noted that the Constitutional Court succeeded in extending access to non-contributory benefits to refugees and asylum seekers. A reform process is also underway with the aim of remedying some of these shortcomings.

As a BRICS country, South Africa seeks to fill social protection coverage gaps and continues building its social protection system through a rights-based approach. The South African system is a good example for emulation in the development of social security systems in the region, be it for middle-income countries, countries with diversity in patterns of employment, relatively high unemployment rates and unequal distributions of income and jobs.

5. References

Deacon, B.; Olivier, M.; Beremauro, R. 2015. Social security and social protection of migrants in South Africa and SADC, Miworc Report No. 8 (Johannesburg, African Centre for Migration & Society, University of the Witwatersrand). Available at: www.miworc.org.za/docs/MiWORC-Report-8.pdf.

Devereux, S. 2010. Building social protection systems in Southern Africa, paper prepared in the framework of the European Report on Development 2010. Available at: http://erd.eui.eu/media/BackgroundPapers/Devereaux%20-%20BUILDING%20SOCIAL%20PROTECTION%20SYSTEMS.pdf.

Government of South Africa. Constitution of the Republic of South Africa, 1996- Chapter 2: Bill of Rights. Available at: www.gov.za/documents/constitution/chapter-2-bill-rights#27.

HelpAge International. 2003. Non-contributory pensions and poverty prevention: A comparative study of Brazil and South Africa (Manchester, Institute for Development Policy and Management/HelpAge).

ILO. 2010. Extending social security to all: A guide through challenges and options (Geneva). Available at: www.ilo.org/wcmsp5/groups/public/@dgreports/@dcomm/@publ/documents/publication/wcms_146616.pdf.

—. n.d. Social protection floors in South Africa. Available at: www.social-protection.org/gimi/gess/ShowWiki.action?wiki.wikiId=852.

International Social Security Association (ISSA). 2008. South Africa. Available at: www.issa.int/aiss/Observatory/Country-Profiles/Regions/Africa/South-Africa#.

Mywage.co.za. Social Security. Available at: www.mywage.co.za/main/decent-work/social-security.

Republic of South Africa. 2014. Report to the Government: Assessment of the South African legislation in view of a possible ratification of the Social Security (Minimum Standards) Convention, 1952 (No. 102) (Geneva, International Labour Office; International Labour Office Decent Work Team for Eastern and Southern African and ILO Country Office for South Africa, Botswana, Lesotho, Namibia and Swaziland).

Republic of South Africa, National Treasury. 2010. Budget Review. Available at: www.treasury.gov.za/documents/national%20budget/2010/revi ew/Budget%20Review.pdf.

UNDP. 2010. "South Africa: Child Support Grants", in United Nations Development Programme (UNDP) and International Labour Organization (ILO) (eds.): Successful Social Protection Floor Experiences. Sharing Innovative Experiences Volume 18 (New York).

Woolard, I.; Harttgen, K.; Klasen, S. 2010. The evolution and impact of social security in South Africa, paper prepared for the Conference on "Promoting Resilience through Social Protection in Sub-Saharan Africa", Dakar, 28-30 June. Available at: http://erd.eui.eu/media/BackgroundPapers/Woolard-Harttgen-Klasen.pdf

18

Thailand: National Health Insurance Registry[27]

Built on a partnership between the Ministry of Interior and social health protection schemes, the national health insurance beneficiary registry facilitates access to health care for all, and ensures that health services better respond to the needs of patients.

Launched in 2001, the Universal Coverage Scheme (UCS) covers all residents not covered by other social health protection schemes, namely the private employees' Social Security Scheme (SSS) and the Civil Servants' Medical Benefit Scheme (CSMBS).

A national registry of beneficiaries has been built based on the population database maintained by the Ministry of Interior (MOI). It is shared by the three social health protection schemes. Identification of UCS beneficiaries is made by removing from this complete database those covered by SSS and CSMBS.

The national identification (ID) number is used by health-care providers to verify eligibility, track delivered services, settle claims, and build a shared medical record for each patient.

---

[27] This chapter was authored by Netnapis Suchonwanich of the National Health Security Office in Thailand, and Thibault van Langenhove of the ILO and reviewed by Thaworn Sakunphanit of the Health Insurance System Research Office in Thailand, and Isabel Ortiz and Valérie Schmitt of the ILO. It was first published in September 2015.

1. Main lessons learned

- Thailand's UCS highlights the importance of national database systems for achieving universal health care. The unique national ID number is used to guarantee that all the population has access to health coverage and monitor utilization of health-care services and financial transactions.
- The use of the national ID numbers has led to improvements in the efficiency and transparency of the national social health protection system's management, as well as prevented misuse of public resources.
- Additional identification systems had to be developed to cover those residents who are not part of the national ID card system, such as minorities and migrant workers.
- The development and maintenance of the shared database system rely on clear cooperation outlined in a memorandum of understanding (MoU) signed by the MOI and the National Health Security Office (NHSO). The Registration of Residential Inhabitant Act, B.E. 2534 (1991), provides the MOI with authority to share data with other government agencies according to their specific missions.

2. Need for a shared database to achieve universal coverage

Despite the gradual extension of health protection coverage in Thailand since the 1970s, at the turn of the millennium it was clear that more needed to be done to improve access to health care and finally achieve universal coverage. In 2001, approximately 30 per cent of the Thai population (18 million people) had no health coverage and would bear the entire burden of health-care costs, although exemptions from the payment of fees were granted by hospitals on a case-by-case basis.

To reach these people, the Universal Coverage Scheme (UCS) was launched in six provinces in April 2001, in an additional 15 provinces in June 2001, and nationwide in April 2002. The principle of the UCS is simple: it aims at covering the 76 per cent of the population not covered by other social health protection schemes, which mainly are (a) the Social Security Scheme (SSS) for private sector employees and (b) the Civil Servant Medical Benefit Scheme (CSMBS) for government employees and government retirees, as well as their spouses, dependants under 20 years old, and parents.

One of the preconditions of the UCS implementation was to be able to identify its beneficiaries and to guarantee all Thai residents have access to one of the existing social health protection schemes.

Figure 22: Characteristics of Thailand's national ID

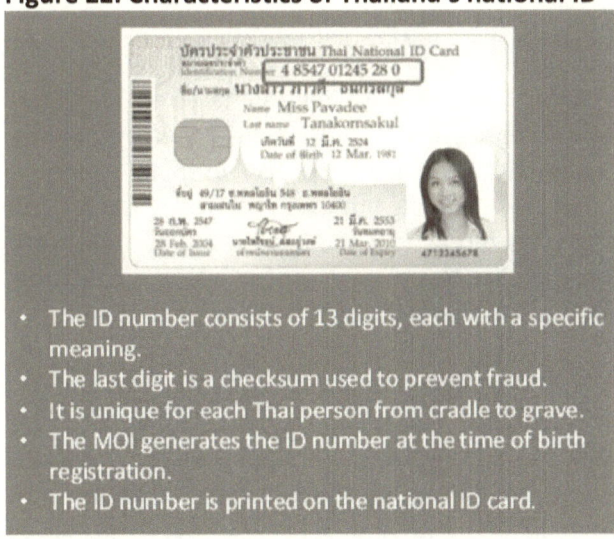

- The ID number consists of 13 digits, each with a specific meaning.
- The last digit is a checksum used to prevent fraud.
- It is unique for each Thai person from cradle to grave.
- The MOI generates the ID number at the time of birth registration.
- The ID number is printed on the national ID card.

3. A registry identifying the beneficiaries thanks to a unique ID number and a health smart card

At the beginning of the UCS implementation the proportion of beneficiaries who were eligible to more than one scheme was high (around 10 per cent). On the contrary, many residents were not registered in any of the existing schemes. The need to identify UCS beneficiaries among Thai residents led to the joint establishment by the three national health social protection schemes of a national health insurance beneficiary registry. The National Health Security Office (NHSO)—an autonomous institution created to manage the UCS—was designated to compile and maintain this registry.

In order to compile a complete registry of all Thai citizens, NHSO uses the national civil registration database, established and maintained by the National Civil Registration Office, Ministry of Interior (MOI). By law, this office is responsible for registering all births, deaths, marriages, divorces, and migrations. A unique 13-digit identification number is generated for each Thai citizen at the time that their births are registered in the national civil registration database. National ID cards are issued to citizens when they reach the age of 7 years old.

National ID numbers are used to register children at school, apply for driving licenses, and request many other documents. Since 2001, national ID numbers are also used to identify a citizen upon delivery of health-care services, track their utilization of services throughout the health-care system, settle claims, and ensure that health-care procedures are consistent across different health-care facilities.

The National Civil Registration Office and the managers of the three health insurance schemes dynamically update the population data on a daily basis by adding births, removing deceased citizens, and recording shifts in memberships across the three schemes. The list of UCS beneficiaries is produced based on the comprehensive MOI Database, excluding SSS and CSMBS beneficiaries.

In accordance with the ILO Social Protection Floors Recommendation, 2012 (No. 202), the UCS is not designed only for Thai people, but for all residents of Thailand. Although the issuance of national ID cards is restricted to Thai people, the MOI still issues national ID numbers for non-Thai residents (the first digit of the ID number identifies that the person is non-Thai). Based on these unique ID numbers, health cards for foreigners are delivered by NHSO at the time of registration. Despite them not being "smart", health cards for foreigners perform similar functions (i.e. identification of the beneficiary, unique ID that can be used to search information in the database, among other functions). For non-Thai people who have not been registered by MOI, NHSO registers them and generates a unique ID number which gives them access to health-care services.

Figure 23: Coverage under social health protection schemes in Thailand, 2001-12

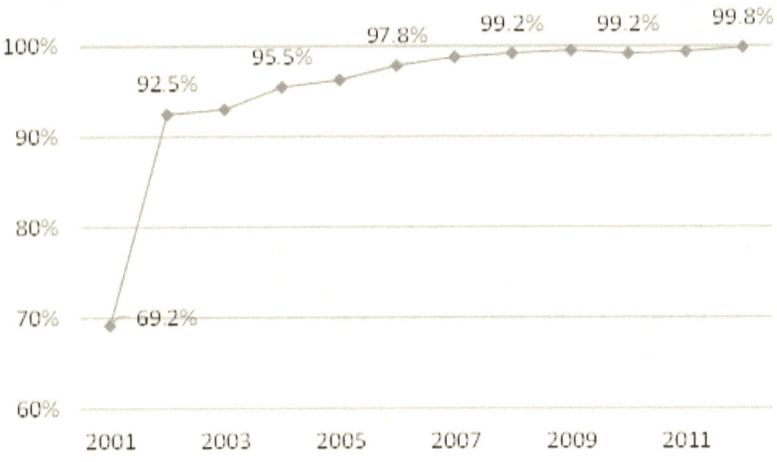

Source: National Health Security Office, 2013.

In addition to the national registry, an administrative database stores information tied to national ID numbers for all outpatient and inpatient care, as well as medical and service transactions. Discharge summaries, claims under diagnosis-related groups, and patients' annual expenditures covered by health social protection schemes are all linked to the patients' unique ID number. Thus, the system can provide for each resident information on the current affiliation status as well as historical transactions across the different social health protection schemes. Upon delivery of services, health-care professionals can access the patient's profile, including their personal medical records. This guarantees that all patients are provided quality health care that responds to their needs.

4. Next steps

Thailand plans to increase the efficiency of the national health-care system by decreasing fraud, human error, and overhead costs. The introduction in 2005 of smart cards for Thai nationals has made fraud virtually impossible. Through increased collaboration between the National Civil Registration Office and the three social health protection schemes it is expected that the health insurance beneficiary registry will be updated on a more frequent basis, allowing for more information to be shared and delays in sharing information reduced.

The close collaboration between NHSO and MOI has led to improvements in Thailand's births and deaths registration system. For example, one project (initiated in 2011) between NHSO, MOI, Ministry of Public Health (MoPH), and UNICEF aims to directly and electronically send information on newborns from the hospital delivery room to MOI's database. This online birth registration system will progressively replace the previous one where parents register their newborns at a district office within 15 days of delivery. The online birth registration system was implemented nationwide in 2013 and is now available in all public hospitals. However, it has not yet been extended to the hospitals/clinics outside the NHSO network.

5. References

Health Insurance System Research Office. 2012. Thailand's Universal Coverage Scheme: achievements and challenges, an independent assessment of the first 10 years (2001-2010) (Nonthaburi).

—.2015. Official website. Available at: www.hisro.or.th.

Ministry of Public Health; Thai Health Promotion Foundation. 2008. Thailand health profile, 2005-2007 (Bangkok, The War Veterans Organization of Thailand).

NHSO. 2015. Official website. Available at: www.nhso.go.th.

Sakunphanit, T. 2008. Universal health care coverage through pluralistic approaches: Experience from Thailand (Bangkok, ILO). Available at:
www.ilo.org/wcmsp5/groups/public/---ed_protect/---soc_sec/documents/publication/wcms_secsoc_6612.pdf.

Scheil-Adlung, X. 2014. Universal Health Protection: Progress to date and the way forward, Social Protection Policy Papers No. 10 (Geneva, ILO). Available at: www.ilo.org/secsoc/information-resources/publications-and-tools/policy-papers/WCMS_305947/lang--en/index.htm.

Schmitt, V.; Sakunphanit, T.; Prasitsiriphol, O. 2013. Social protection assessment based national dialogue: Towards a nationally defined social protection floor in Thailand (Bangkok, ILO). Available at:
www.social-protection.org/gimi/gess/ShowProjectRessource.action?ressource.ressourceId=38377&pid=2097.

Tessier, L. 2014. "Thailand: Universal Health Coverage", in Social protection in action: Innovative experiences (Geneva, ILO). Available at:
www.social-protection.org/gimi/gess/RessourcePDF.action?ressource.ressourceId=44142.

19

Uruguay: Instilling a culture of social protection[28]

In 2007, Uruguay launched an education initiative on social security which aims to inform the population of their rights and obligations, promote active participation in the improvement of the social security system and extend its coverage. The Programme is part of a comprehensive approach to build a fairer society and ensure decent lives for all.

Through a joint effort between the Social Security Institution (BPS) and the institutions responsible for education and culture, the Government of Uruguay introduced content on social security to the curricula used in all schools and professional training institutions at all levels.

To date, a programme called "Know Your Rights and Obligations to Social Security" reaches 100 per cent of students, including children from 5 years of age, adolescents attending high school and adults attending vocational training institutions or finalizing formal studies.

Uruguay has demonstrated that creating a culture of social security constitutes an important tool to extend social security and improve its functioning.

---

[28] This chapter was authored by Eduardo Méndez of the Banco de Previsón Social in Uruguay, and Victoria Giroud of the ILO and reviewed by Isabel Ortiz, Fabio Durán-Valverde and Valérie Schmitt of the ILO. It was first published in August 2016.

1. Main lessons learned

- The development of a culture of social protection contributes to coverage extension.
- Building culture is a country-specific process concerning society as a whole and relying on strong political will.
- The "Know Your Rights and Obligations to Social Security" programme is part of a three pillar strategy: education; public awareness raising; and training staff working in the social security institution. This strategy ensures sufficient institutional capacity to respond to well-informed and active beneficiaries.
- The Programme is compulsory and it has been implemented progressively in all public and private schools. It reaches all children, adolescents and adults attending learning institutions starting from the age of 5.
- Formal agreements between the Social Security Institution and institutions in the areas of education and culture guaranteed the development of the programme and its sustainability.
- Teachers, students and social security experts participated in the pedagogical design and development of the training manuals. This process ensured the appropriation and continuous improvement of the materials.

2. Why was the programme implemented?

In Uruguay, the Social Security Institution plans, coordinates and administers social security according to International Labour Organization conventions and recommendations, particularly the Social Security (Minimum Standards) Convention, 1952 (No. 102), and the Social Protection Floors Recommendation, 2012 (No. 202). Currently, 97 per cent of people above 65 years old receive a pension and 87 per cent of jobs are in the formal economy.

In 2005, the Government of Uruguay implemented public policies to extend social protection to the vulnerable and poor populations. Fieldwork showed that hundreds of individuals who qualified for social protection benefits did not have access due to a lack of knowledge and information. The Government developed and implemented a social security education programme based on the belief that the main obstacle to exercise the right to social protection was a lack of knowledge.

The Uruguayan constitution guarantees free and non-religious education for the entire population. The mandatory educational period totals 14 years and the literacy rate is 98 per cent. This is a key factor in guaranteeing the development of a social security culture through the education system.

The "Know Your Rights and Obligations to Social Security" programme started its activities in 2006 as a result of having a universal social protection system and a sound education system.

The Programme is based on two key convictions: (i) exercising a right and fulfilling its inherent obligations relies on having knowledge of that right; and (ii) the social construction of the social protection system can only be achieved through the active participation of citizens.

"In the field of social security education and training, programmes and actions should be coordinated with the Ministry of Education and Culture, the National Administration of Public Education, the University of the Eastern Republic of Uruguay and the Vocational School, as well as with private education institutions and international organizations."

Strategic Plan – Social Security Institution-BPS 2005-2010

---

3. A culture of social security: Towards universal social protection?

Uruguay had already achieved universal legal coverage for social security at the start of the Programme. However, many Uruguayans were not informed of their rights. The Programme has contributed to making the right to social security a reality.

The Programme is based on the following convictions:
- Citizenship is exercised by every social group, by all actors and at every age.
- Education and information are the most powerful instruments for social change.
- Social security institutions should have the capacity to respond efficiently to the requirements of beneficiaries.

Consequently, the programme strategy relies on three axes that are linked and mutually reinforcing:
- education for children and teenagers in educational environments through the "Know Your Rights and Obligations to Social Security" programme;
- public information and communication campaigns; and
- capacity building for Social Security Institution staff.

4. The "Know Your Rights and Obligations to Social Security" programme

The Programme arises as a result of institutional agreements between the Social Security Institution and the National

Administration of Public Education. These agreements formalize the use of the education system to introduce social security as a mandatory subject within curricula delivered at all public and private schools.

Interdisciplinary teams of teachers and Social Security Institution technical staff gradually developed the training manuals starting in 2006. Students also participated in the design, development and validation of the training manuals.

The main contents of the manuals are detailed as follows:
- the concept of social protection as a fundamental human right;
- solidarity and responsibility as main values;
- the implementation of solidarity through social security contributions and benefits; and
- the Social Security Institution (BPS) as the state body responsible for the administration of the social security system.

The educational materials were designed to be addressed from different areas of study and perspectives according to the age of the students, including through civic education, mathematics (calculations of contributions) and biology (health, maternity and prevention). Students' learning outcomes on social security are evaluated. Teachers attend capacity building sessions based on specific training materials.

School cycle	Manuals
Preschool (5 to 6 years old)	Growing up together
Primary education (7 to 11 years old)	Interactive notebook: Know your rights and obligations to social security
High school – first cycle (12 to 15 years old)	Manual 1: Know your rights and obligations on social security
High school – second	Manual 2: Know your rights and

cycle and professional training (16 to 19 years old)	obligations to social security
Non-formal education (non-age bound)	Manual 3: Know your rights and obligations on social security

The Social Security Institution's Centre of Studies on Social Security is responsible for coordinating the implementation and monitoring of the Programme.

The Programme is financed by the Social Security Institution and the National Administration of Public Education. Both institutions include the programme costs in their human resources budgets. The Social Security Institution covers printing costs and the National Post Administration delivers the manuals free of charge.

5. Impact of the education programme on the population

As a result of Uruguay's public and economic policies, the coverage of social security has increased gradually since 2005. The social security culture resulting from the implementation of the education programme is one of the key factors that has contributed to the extension of coverage. Between the start of the programme in 2006 and 2014, the number of people registered for social security increased by 22 per cent and the amount of pension benefits grew by 15 per cent.

The "Know Your Rights and Obligations to Social Security" programme has delivered 1.2 million manuals through the education system and professional training institutions. In an effort to make the content accessible to everyone, braille versions of the first three manuals have been produced for students with visual impairments.

The impact of the Programme goes beyond the students as it impacts the family as a whole. Evaluation studies highlight positive outcomes and point out that the Programme's main goals are being reached through its appropriation by the education system, institutions and students.

Figure 24: Contributions and benefits for social security in Uruguay, 2007-14

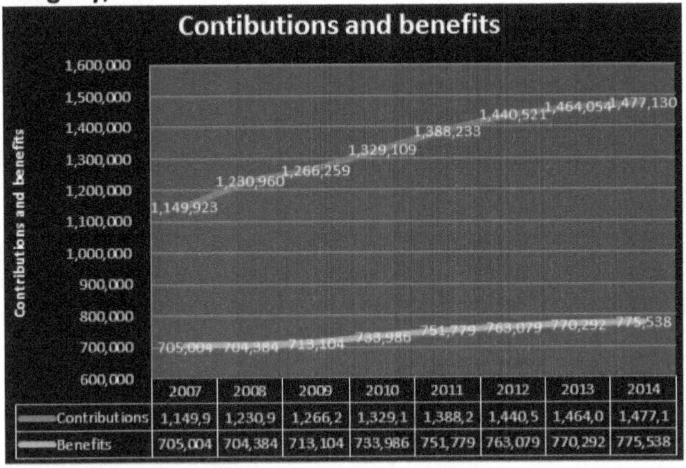

	2007	2008	2009	2010	2011	2012	2013	2014
Contributions	1,149,9	1,230,9	1,266,2	1,329,1	1,388,2	1,440,5	1,464,0	1,477,1
Benefits	705,004	704,384	713,104	733,986	751,779	763,079	770,292	775,538

At the international level, the Uruguayan experience provides a model for other countries. Several international organizations, such as the International Labour Organization, the International Conference on Social Security and the Ibero-American Social Security Organization, have invited Uruguay to present their experiences with the Programme at international events and South-South exchanges. Likewise, several countries have requested support from Uruguay to design their own education programmes to develop a social security culture.

6. Main challenges

To date, the "Know Your Rights and Obligations to Social Security" programme is well-consolidated, institutionalized and integrated. It follows a permanent extension process. The most important challenge for the programme is long-term sustainability.

In the coming years, the Programme should evolve and change to support structural changes that impact the social security system. The Programme should also be ready to face new challenges, such as the aging of the population, strong international migration flows, increasing unemployment and climate and environmental chan...

7. References

Bertranou, F.; Gammage, S.; Saravia, L. 2012. Educación en seguridad social. Reflexiones a partir de la experiencia internacional (documento preliminar) (Santiago, ILO).

BPS. Plan estratégico 2005-2010 (Montevideo, BPS). Available at: www.bps.gub.uy.

—; CEIP; ANEP Correo Uruguayo. 2016. Conoce tus derechos y obligaciones en seguridad social. Manuales y cuaderno interactivo. Available at: www.bps.gub.uy/3374/educacion-en-seguridad-social.html.

Méndez E. 2016. Taller sobre cultura en seguridad social. Buenas prácticas de América Latina para el mundo. Lima, Perú (Montevideo, BPS). Available at: www.social-protection.org/gimi/gess/RessourcePDF.action?ressource.ressourceId=53640.

—. Forthcoming. Cultura en seguridad social. El programa "Conoce tus derechos y obligaciones" de Uruguay (Montevideo, BPS; Geneva, ILO).

Plan Ceibal. Available at: www.ceibal.edu.uy/.

20

Zambia: Financing social protection through taxation of natural resources[29]

Zambia is an example of how countries with rich natural resources can rely on taxation, specifically on natural resource extracting companies, to improve social protection services and programmes and to help mitigate inequality and reduce poverty.

Developing countries often struggle to generate government revenues for social protection through taxation and social security contributions. Tax authorities tend to be weak and taxation lacks transparency. Furthermore, a relatively large share of the population is employed in the informal sector, making it difficult and costly to collect social security contributions or tax employees. This limits the means to redistribute income and to develop adequate social protection systems, including floors, to reduce poverty and inequality.

1. Main lessons learned

- Natural resource-rich countries can boost their social protection system through taxing extractive industries and using the increased government revenues to support the expansion of social protection.
- Through strengthening the tax collection authority and the revenue collection framework of the Government,

[29] This chapter was authored by Stefan Urban of the ILO and reviewed by Isabel Ortiz and Hiroshi Yamabana of the ILO. It was first published in August 2016.

> reduced tax leakages can contribute to further increases in government revenues and the creation of fiscal space for social protection measures.

- In 2013, Zambia's extractive revenues were US$1.5 billion annually and represented 30 per cent of total government revenues.
- With the help of extractive industry revenues, the Government substantially increased the budget for social cash transfer schemes from 55 million Zambian Kwachas (ZMW) in 2012 to ZMW199.2 million in 2014.

2. Natural resource extraction tax in developing countries

Countries with significant reserves of non-renewable natural resources have the potential to collect substantial taxes from the sector to support socio-economic development. A government may either directly extract natural resources through state-owned enterprises or joint-ventures, or sell the exploitation rights and tax profits, both of which provide revenues for social investments. A number of developing and emerging economies have effectively managed their natural resources through public companies, including Botswana (diamonds), Brazil (oil), Indonesia (oil and gas) and Malaysia (forestry, tin, oil and gas).

Environmental and social externalities, such as the impact on local communities, which, if not adequately addressed, can serve as a subsidy to extracting companies and distort the true cost of exploitation. Natural resources from a property rights perspective are resources that ought to be accrued to the public at large rather than to private individuals. Revenues generated from natural resources should be distributed among the society, leaving enough rewards to attract companies to engage in exploitation, while taking into account the true cost of exploitation and equity concerns.

3. Natural resource taxation in Zambia

Zambia is a prominent example of a country using taxes on mineral resources to generate significant government revenues to be used to fund social expenditures. Zambia, with a population of 16.2 million, is the 8th largest producer of copper (2013) and the 9th largest producer of cobalt (2012), with the mining sector accounting for 9 per cent of GDP and 77 per cent (2015) of exports.

In 2013, Zambia's extractive revenues were US$1.5 billion, representing 30 per cent of total government revenues.

While the pre-2008 period is characterized by generous concessions for private sector companies and ineffective management under state ownership, Zambia introduced various measures to increase efficiency and to widen the base for its government revenues. Zambia implemented institutional reforms, such as the creation of a large taxpayers' office and a gradual strengthening of its revenue collection framework. Tax administration today is relatively effective and it experiences significantly lower levels of tax leakages compared with other African countries (Chamber of Mines of Zambia and ICMM, 2014).

The Mines and Minerals Act 2008 is a key piece of legislation that paved the way for this paradigm shift. The legislation introduced the following:
- A graduated windfall tax was levied at a rate of 25 per cent on gross proceeds when the copper price exceeds $2.50 per pound; 50 per cent when the copper price exceeds $3.00 per pound; and 75 per cent in excess of $3.50 per pound. The windfall tax, however, was withdrawn in 2009, largely due to the effects of the financial crisis of 2008.
- The royalty rate was increased to 3 per cent and, since 2012, is set at 6 per cent.

Figure 25: Zambia's fiscal revenues from the mining sector, 1995–2012

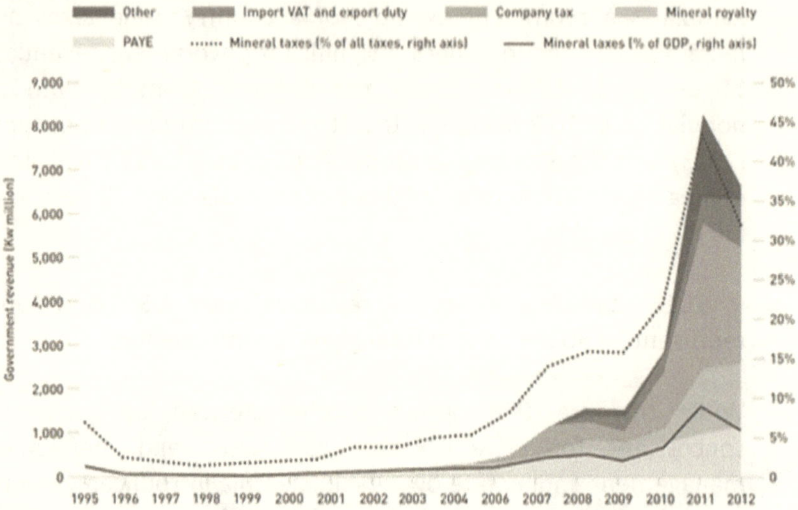

Source: ICMM, 2014, based on original data from the Zambia Revenue Authority.

- The corporate income tax rate for natural extractive industries was increased from 25 to 30 per cent. Simultaneously, the rate for non-mining sectors was reduced from 35 to 30 per cent.
- A new variable profit tax rate was implemented, under which the marginal tax rate would rise from 30 per cent to 45 per cent when taxable profits exceed 8 per cent of gross revenues.
- A withholding tax on interest, royalties, management fees and payments to affiliates or subcontractors for all mining companies was reintroduced and set at a standard rate of 15 per cent. Capital allowances were reduced from 100 per cent of expenses to a conventional 25 per cent per annum (and deductible only in the year production commences rather than in the year when the expense is incurred).
- Hedging as a risk management mechanism is treated as a separate activity from mining.

Abolition of the windfall tax is an example of the political economy implications. The tax was introduced in 2008 and abolished the year after in the aftermath of the global financial crisis and as a result of increased threats by transnational corporations to lower investments, close mines and take legal action against the measures. Table 2 summarizes the main shifts in the taxation of natural extractive industries.

Table 2: Taxation of natural extractive industries in Zambia, 2006 and 2010

Measure/Year	2006	2010
Royalty	0.6%	6%
Corporate income tax	25%	30%
Variable income tax	No	Yes
Windfall tax	No	No*
Custom duties	Exports=0	15% for unprocessed copper
Income of foreign subcontractors and interest	0%	15%

*Introduced in 2008, but abolished after the global financial crisis. Source: Simpasa et al., 2013, based on Zambia Revenue Authority and IMF, 2012.

Additional legislation aimed at curtailing capital flight and the underreporting of mineral earnings was enacted in 2013 by the Zambian Government. The law applies to all international transactions, including profits, dividends, remittances, loans to non-residents and investments abroad by persons resident in Zambia.

Among mining countries (excluding petroleum) world-wide, Zambia's mining receipts are the second highest after Botswana, and higher than revenues of Chile, Democratic Republic of Congo or Guinea.

In the year after the introduction of the 2008 Act, tax collection from the mining sector did not meet expectations, with an increase from ZMW1.1 billion in 2007 to ZMW1.5 billion in 2008. The main reasons for this result were delays in tax payments due to disputes concerning the Act, combined with a fall in copper production due to the worldwide crisis. Since then, government revenues have improved considerably, from less than ZMW1 billion per year before 2008 to ZMW6.619 billion in 2012.

4. Natural resource taxation and social protection

The Government of Zambia emphasises health, education and social protection as means to achieve their developmental goals. The 2014 budget confirms the increased spending on these areas. As illustrated in Table 3, the Government increased its spending on health, education and social protection from ZMW8,086 million (29.2 per cent of total budget) in 2011 to ZMW14,018 million (32.9 per cent) in 2013.

Furthermore, the Government increased the budget for social cash transfer schemes substantially, from ZMW55 million in 2012 to ZMW199.2 million in 2014. These substantial shifts in social protection spending can be linked to both a change in leadership as well as to an improved fiscal position that was achieved through significantly increased government revenues from natural resource taxation.

The Government has taken steps towards developing a social protection policy with rights-based entitlements and creating additional fiscal space for social protection by abolishing fuel and maize miller subsidies. Former social protection programmes which distributed benefits to people in return for political favours have been reformed into more structured and transparent programmes.

Table 3: Total social expenditure by the Government in Zambia, 2011-13

	2011		2012		2013	
	in million ZMK	% of budget	in million ZMK	% of budget	in million ZMK	% of budget
Health	2,579.9	9.3%	3,638.1	11.3%	4,228.4	9.9%
Education	4,850.5	17.5%	5,626.8	17.5%	8,607.0	20.2%
Social protection	655.6	2.4%	892.2	2.8%	1,183.0	2.8%
Total	8,086	29.2%	10,157.1	31.6%	14,018.4	32.9%

5. Conclusion

The case of Zambia shows that resource-rich developing countries can substantially expand fiscal space for social protection and other socio-economic expenditures. Taxing natural resource extracting industries allowed the Zambian Government to improve their fiscal position and created the basis for the expansion of their social protection system.

Taxing natural resource extraction is one of the many alternatives to expand fiscal space for social protection. Governments normally use a mix of taxes and social security contributions to fund social protection, combined with other options explained in the paper, "Fiscal space for social protection: Options to expand social investments in 187 countries".

6. References

Boadway, R; Flatters, F. 1993. The taxation of natural resources – Principles and policy issues, Policy Research working papers No. WPS 1210 (Washington, DC, World Bank).

Ernst, C. Forthcoming. Revenues from extractive industries: An opportunity to finance sustainable social spending (Geneva, International Labour Organization).

Zambia Extractive Industries Transparency Initiative. 2015. Seventh report of the Zambia extractive industries transparency initiative (ZEITI), for the year ended 31 December 2014 (Lusaka, BDO East Africa & BDO Zambia).

Kuss, M.K. 2015. The prospects and politics of social protection reform in Zambia, IDS Working Paper Volume 2015, No. 453, CSP Working Paper Number 11 (Brighton, Centre for Social Protection, Institute of Development Studies).

Ortiz, I.; Cummins, M.; Karunanethy, K. 2015. Fiscal space for social protection: Options to expand social investments in 187 countries, ESS Working Paper No. 48 (Geneva, International Labour Office).

Simpasa, A.; Hailu, D.; Levin, S; Tibana, R.J. 2013. Capturing mineral revenues in Zambia: Past trends and future prospects (New York, United Nations Development Programme & EU-UN Global Partnership on Land, Natural Resources and Conflict).

Chamber of Mines of Zambia. 2014. Enhancing mining`s contribution to the Zambian economy and society (London, International Council on Mining & Metals (ICMM)).

Annex 1: Social Protection Floors Recommendation, 2012 (No. 202)

PREAMBLE

The General Conference of the International Labour Organization,

Having been convened at Geneva by the Governing Body of the International Labour Office, and having met in its 101st Session on 30 May 2012, and

Reaffirming that the right to social security is a human right, and

Acknowledging that the right to social security is, along with promoting employment, an economic and social necessity for development and progress, and

Recognizing that social security is an important tool to prevent and reduce poverty, inequality, social exclusion and social insecurity, to promote equal opportunity and gender and racial equality, and to support the transition from informal to formal employment, and

Considering that social security is an investment in people that empowers them to adjust to changes in the economy and in the labour market, and that social security systems act as automatic social and economic stabilizers, help stimulate aggregate demand in times of crisis and beyond, and help support a transition to a more sustainable economy, and

Considering that the prioritization of policies aimed at sustainable long-term growth associated with social inclusion helps overcome extreme poverty and reduces social inequalities and differences within and among regions, and

Recognizing that the transition to formal employment and the establishment of sustainable social security systems are mutually supportive, and

Recalling that the Declaration of Philadelphia recognizes the solemn obligation of the International Labour Organization to contribute to "achiev[ing] ... the extension of social security measures to provide a basic income to all in need of such protection and comprehensive medical care", and

Considering the Universal Declaration of Human Rights, in particular Articles 22 and 25, and the International Covenant on Economic, Social and Cultural Rights, in particular Articles 9, 11 and 12, and

Considering also ILO social security standards, in particular the Social Security (Minimum Standards) Convention, 1952 (No. 102), the Income Security Recommendation, 1944 (No. 67), and the Medical Care Recommendation, 1944 (No. 69), and noting that these standards are of continuing relevance and continue to be important references for social security systems, and

Recalling that the ILO Declaration on Social Justice for a Fair Globalization recognizes that "the commitments and efforts of Members and the Organization to implement the ILO's constitutional mandate, including through international labour standards, and to place full and productive employment and decent work at the centre of economic and social policies, should be based on ... (ii) developing and enhancing measures of social protection ... which are sustainable and adapted to national circumstances, including ... the extension of social security to all", and

Considering the resolution and Conclusions concerning the recurrent discussion on social protection (social security) adopted by the International Labour Conference at its 100th Session (2011), which recognize the need for a Recommendation complementing existing ILO social security standards and providing guidance to Members in building social protection floors tailored to national circumstances and levels of development, as part of comprehensive social security systems, and

Having decided upon the adoption of certain proposals with regard to social protection floors, which are the subject of the fourth item on the agenda of the session, and

Having determined that these proposals shall take the form of a Recommendation; adopts this fourteenth day of June of the year two thousand and twelve the following Recommendation, which may be cited as the Social Protection Floors Recommendation, 2012.

I. OBJECTIVES, SCOPE AND PRINCIPLES

1. This Recommendation provides guidance to Members to:
   a. establish and maintain, as applicable, social protection floors as a fundamental element of their national social security systems; and
   b. implement social protection floors within strategies for the extension of social security that progressively ensure higher levels of social security to as many people as possible, guided by ILO social security standards.
2. For the purpose of this Recommendation, social protection floors are nationally defined sets of basic social security guarantees which secure protection aimed at preventing or alleviating poverty, vulnerability and social exclusion.
3. Recognizing the overall and primary responsibility of the State in giving effect to this Recommendation, Members should apply the following principles:
   a. universality of protection, based on social solidarity;
   b. entitlement to benefits prescribed by national law;
   c. adequacy and predictability of benefits;
   d. non-discrimination, gender equality and responsiveness to special needs;
   e. social inclusion, including of persons in the informal economy;
   f. respect for the rights and dignity of people covered by the social security guarantees;
   g. progressive realization, including by setting targets and time frames;
   h. solidarity in financing while seeking to achieve an optimal balance between the responsibilities and interests among those who finance and benefit from social security schemes;
   i. consideration of diversity of methods and approaches, including of financing mechanisms and delivery systems;

    j.   transparent, accountable and sound financial management and administration;

    k.   financial, fiscal and economic sustainability with due regard to social justice and equity;

    l.   coherence with social, economic and employment policies;

    m. coherence across institutions responsible for delivery of social protection;

    n.   high-quality public services that enhance the delivery of social security systems;

    o.   efficiency and accessibility of complaint and appeal procedures;

    p.   regular monitoring of implementation, and periodic evaluation;

    q.   full respect for collective bargaining and freedom of association for all workers; and

    r.   tripartite participation with representative organizations of employers and workers, as well as consultation with other relevant and representative organizations of persons concerned.

II. NATIONAL SOCIAL PROTECTION FLOORS

4.   Members should, in accordance with national circumstances, establish as quickly as possible and maintain their social protection floors comprising basic social security guarantees. The guarantees should ensure at a minimum that, over the life cycle, all in need have access to essential health care and to basic income security which together secure effective access to goods and services defined as necessary at the national level.

5.   The social protection floors referred to in Paragraph 4 should comprise at least the following basic social security guarantees:

    a.   access to a nationally defined set of goods and services, constituting essential health care, including maternity care, that meets the criteria of availability, accessibility, acceptability and quality;

    b.   basic income security for children, at least at a nationally defined minimum level, providing access to nutrition, education, care and any other necessary goods and services;

    c.   basic income security, at least at a nationally defined minimum level, for persons in active age who are unable to earn sufficient income, in particular in cases of sickness, unemployment, maternity and disability; and

    d.   basic income security, at least at a nationally defined minimum level, for older persons.

6.   Subject to their existing international obligations, Members should provide the basic social security guarantees referred to in this Recommendation to at least all residents and children, as defined in national laws and regulations.

7.   Basic social security guarantees should be established by law. National laws and regulations should specify the range, qualifying conditions and levels of the benefits giving effect to these guarantees. Impartial, transparent, effective, simple, rapid, accessible and inexpensive complaint and appeal procedures should also be specified. Access to complaint and appeal procedures should be free of charge to the applicant. Systems should be in place that enhance compliance with national legal frameworks.

8.   When defining the basic social security guarantees, Members should give due consideration to the following:

    a.   persons in need of health care should not face hardship and an increased risk of poverty due to the financial consequences of accessing essential health care. Free prenatal and postnatal medical care for the most vulnerable should also be considered;

    b.   basic income security should allow life in dignity. Nationally defined minimum levels of income may correspond to the monetary value of a set of necessary goods and services, national poverty lines, income thresholds for social assistance or other comparable thresholds established by national law or practice, and may take into account regional differences;

    c.   the levels of basic social security guarantees should be regularly reviewed through a transparent procedure that is established by national laws, regulations or practice, as appropriate; and

    d.   in regard to the establishment and review of the levels of these guarantees, tripartite participation with representative organizations of employers and workers, as well as consultation with other relevant and representative organizations of persons concerned, should be ensured.

9.

    1.   In providing the basic social security guarantees, Members should consider different approaches with a view to implementing the most effective and efficient combination of benefits and schemes in the national context.

    2.   Benefits may include child and family benefits, sickness and health-care benefits, maternity benefits, disability benefits, old-age benefits, survivors' benefits, unemployment benefits and employment guarantees, and employment injury benefits as well as any other social benefits in cash or in kind.

    3.   Schemes providing such benefits may include universal benefit schemes, social insurance schemes, social assistance schemes, negative income tax schemes, public employment schemes and employment support schemes.

10. In designing and implementing national social protection floors, Members should:

    a.   combine preventive, promotional and active measures, benefits and social services;

    b.   promote productive economic activity and formal employment through considering policies that include public procurement, government credit provisions, labour inspection, labour market policies and tax incentives, and that promote education, vocational training, productive skills and employability; and

    c. ensure coordination with other policies that enhance formal employment, income generation, education, literacy, vocational training, skills and employability, that reduce precariousness, and that promote secure work, entrepreneurship and sustainable enterprises within a decent work framework.

11.

    1. Members should consider using a variety of different methods to mobilize the necessary resources to ensure financial, fiscal and economic sustainability of national social protection floors, taking into account the contributory capacities of different population groups. Such methods may include, individually or in combination, effective enforcement of tax and contribution obligations, reprioritizing expenditure, or a broader and sufficiently progressive revenue base.

    2. In applying such methods, Members should consider the need to implement measures to prevent fraud, tax evasion and non-payment of contributions.

12. National social protection floors should be financed by national resources. Members whose economic and fiscal capacities are insufficient to implement the guarantees may seek international cooperation and support that complement their own efforts.

III. NATIONAL STRATEGIES FOR THE EXTENSION OF SOCIAL SECURITY

13.

    1. Members should formulate and implement national social security extension strategies, based on national consultations through effective social dialogue and social participation. National strategies should:

        a. prioritize the implementation of social protection floors as a starting point for countries that do not have a minimum level of social security guarantees, and as a fundamental element of their national social security systems; and

       b. seek to provide higher levels of protection to as many people as possible, reflecting economic and fiscal capacities of Members, and as soon as possible.

    2. For this purpose, Members should progressively build and maintain comprehensive and adequate social security systems coherent with national policy objectives and seek to coordinate social security policies with other public policies.

14. When formulating and implementing national social security extension strategies, Members should:

    a. set objectives reflecting national priorities;

    b. identify gaps in, and barriers to, protection;

    c. seek to close gaps in protection through appropriate and effectively coordinated schemes, whether contributory or non-contributory, or both, including through the extension of existing contributory schemes to all concerned persons with contributory capacity;

    d. complement social security with active labour market policies, including vocational training or other measures, as appropriate;

    e. specify financial requirements and resources as well as the time frame and sequencing for the progressive achievement of the objectives; and

    f. raise awareness about their social protection floors and their extension strategies, and undertake information programmes, including through social dialogue.

15. Social security extension strategies should apply to persons both in the formal and informal economy and support the growth of formal employment and the reduction of informality, and should be consistent with, and conducive to, the implementation of the social, economic and environmental development plans of Members.

16. Social security extension strategies should ensure support for disadvantaged groups and people with special needs.

17. When building comprehensive social security systems reflecting national objectives, priorities and economic and fiscal capacities, Members should aim to achieve the range

and levels of benefits set out in the Social Security (Minimum Standards) Convention, 1952 (No. 102), or in other ILO social security Conventions and Recommendations setting out more advanced standards.

18. Members should consider ratifying, as early as national circumstances allow, the Social Security (Minimum Standards) Convention, 1952 (No. 102). Furthermore, Members should consider ratifying, or giving effect to, as applicable, other ILO social security Conventions and Recommendations setting out more advanced standards.

IV. MONITORING

19. Members should monitor progress in implementing social protection floors and achieving other objectives of national social security extension strategies through appropriate nationally defined mechanisms, including tripartite participation with representative organizations of employers and workers, as well as consultation with other relevant and representative organizations of persons concerned.

20. Members should regularly convene national consultations to assess progress and discuss policies for the further horizontal and vertical extension of social security.

21. For the purpose of Paragraph 19, Members should regularly collect, compile, analyse and publish an appropriate range of social security data, statistics and indicators, disaggregated, in particular, by gender.

22. In developing or revising the concepts, definitions and methodology used in the production of social security data, statistics and indicators, Members should take into consideration relevant guidance provided by the International Labour Organization, in particular, as appropriate, the resolution concerning the development of social security statistics adopted by the Ninth International Conference of Labour Statisticians.

23. Members should establish a legal framework to secure and protect private individual information contained in their social security data systems.

24.

1. Members are encouraged to exchange information, experiences and expertise on social security strategies, policies and practices among themselves and with the International Labour Office.

2. In implementing this Recommendation, Members may seek technical assistance from the International Labour Organization and other relevant international organizations in accordance with their respective mandates.

Annex 2: Sustainable Development Goals related to social protection

Goal 1
End poverty in all its forms everywhere
Target 1.3
Implement nationally appropriate social protection systems and measures for all, including floors, and by 2030 achieve substantial coverage of the poor and the vulnerable

Goal 3
Ensure healthy lives and promote well-being for all at all ages
Target 3.8
Achieve universal health coverage, including financial risk protection, access to quality essential health-care services and access to safe, effective, quality and affordable essential medicines and vaccines for all

Goal 5
Achieve gender equality and empower all women and girls
Target 5.4
Recognize and value unpaid care and domestic work through the provision of public services, infrastructure and social protection policies and the promotion of shared responsibility within the household and the family as nationally appropriate

Goal 8
Promote sustained, inclusive and sustainable economic growth, full and productive employment and decent work for all
Target 8.5
By 2030, achieve full and productive employment and decent work for all women and men, including for young people and persons with disabilities, and equal pay for work of equal value

Goal 10
Reduce inequality within and among countries
Target 10.4
Adopt policies, especially fiscal, wage and social protection policies, and progressively achieve greater equality

Annex 3: ILO standards on social protection

The up-to-date ILO Conventions and Recommendations on social security or social protection are listed below:

- The Social Security (Minimum Standards) Convention, 1952 (No. 102), which covers all nine branches of social security and sets minimum standards for these nine branches;
- The Income Security Recommendation, 1944 (No. 67) and the Medical Care Recommendation, 1944 (No. 69) , which envisage comprehensive social security systems and the extension of coverage to all and laid the foundations for Convention No. 102 (1952).

Other up-to-date Conventions and Recommendations, adopted after Convention No. 102 (1952), set out higher standards for particular branches of social security. Drawn up on the model of Convention No. 102, they offer a higher level of protection, both in terms of the population covered and of the level of benefits, as follows:

- The Medical Care and Sickness Benefits Convention, 1969 (No. 130) and the Medical Care and Sickness Benefits Recommendation, 1969 (No. 134) makes provision for medical care and sickness benefit;
- The Employment Promotion and Protection against Unemployment Convention, 1988 (No. 168) and the Employment Promotion and Protection against Unemployment Recommendation, 1988 (No. 176) relates to unemployment benefit;
- The Invalidity, Old-Age and Survivors' Benefits Convention, 1967 (No. 128) and the Invalidity, Old-Age and Survivors' Benefits Recommendation, 1967 (No. 131) covers old-age benefit, invalidity benefit and survivor's benefit;

- The Employment Injury Benefits Convention, 1964 (No. 121) and the Employment Injury Benefits Recommendation, 1964 (No. 121) makes provision for employment injury benefit;
- The Maternity Protection Convention, 2000, (No. 183) and the Maternity Protection Recommendation, 2000 (No. 191) covers maternity benefit;
- The Equality of Treatment (Social Security) Convention, 1962 (No. 118), the Maintenance of Social Security Rights Convention, 1982 (No. 157) and the Maintenance of Social Security Rights Recommendation, 1983 (No. 167) provide reinforced protection to migrant workers; and
- The Social Protection Floors Recommendation (No. 202) provides guidance for the establishment and maintenance of social protection floors and their implementation within strategies for the extension of social security aiming at achieving comprehensive social security system.

These instruments can be consulted in the Database of International Labour Standards. (NORMLEX)